D1433209

THE GOLDEN AGE OF FOOD

from around Great Britain & Ireland

This Book is dedicated to the memory of Francis Coulson MBE

THE GOLDEN AGE OF FOOD

from around Great Britain & Ireland

TOM BRIDGE

First published in the United Kingdom in 1999
by Waterton Press Limited

Text & Design Copyright © Waterton Press Limited

All rights reserved. No photograph in this publication may be sold to a third party other
than in the original form of this publication, or framed for sale to a third party.
No parts of this publication may be reproduced, stored in a retrieval system, or transmitted,
in any form, or by any other means, electronic, mechanical, photocopying, recording or
otherwise, without the prior permission of the publishers and copywrite holder.

British Library Cataloguing in Publication Data.

Tom Bridge
The Golden Age of Food from Around Great Britain & Ireland

ISBN 1-84125-300-6

Historical photographs copyright and reproduced by Waterton Press Limited
courtesy of The Francis Frith Collection, Teffont, Salisbury.

Typeset in New Baskerville

Printed and bound in Great Britain by
WBC Book Manufacturers, Bridgend, South Wales

Contents

Barry Island, Wales, 1910.

Acknowledgments

Taking a year of my life to create this book was an experience I will remember with happiness and a feeling of pride. I am proud to have met the following people, without who's help and understanding of British and Irish food this book would not have been possible. Every person involved lived the words *British* and *Irish*. Being a British chef and writer of British food is not enough for me. The people who are involved in the food industry every day, who put their heart and soul into promoting and encouraging us to buy the finest produce in the world, which is on our doorsteps, are the people I admire.

I would like to thank the following, who agree with me that we produce some of the finest food and recipes in the world. The Olverson family for giving Britain Red Velvet beetroot (the most under-rated vegetable), especially Brian, Yo Yo, Bre and Amanda. Sue and Peter Vickers for introducing me to Red Velvet. Oliver and Peter Kay at Rediveg and Openshaws in Bolton. Sam and Pat Clarke for their advice on pickling. Arthur Cunynghame, the only person who can talk cheese 24 hours a day. Sue Webb, McNeils, McCartney's Family butchers (and their award winning sausages and white pudding) of Main Street, Moira, County Down, Northern Ireland. Paul Christopher Glynn and all the Glynn family in Dublin. Brian Sack MBE and everyone at the Sharrow Bay Country House in Ullswater. David Hinds,

Jeremy Roberts and that *'foryn fella'*. Tim Bacon at Life Restaurants. Ann and Pat Gallagher, of Gallaghers at Little Scotland, Blackrod, Lancashire. Bob Burns, a truer cross between Irish and Liverpudlian I have never seen, and everyone at Endmore Ltd. Stan Berwick, who is "Mr Blackpool Tower". Russell Holdsworth at Fayre Game. Maureen and Brigette at the British Academy of Film and Television Arts. My old buddy Ted Weaver, commonly known as "Mr GTA". Betty Duffin at Pines in Clayton le Woods. Michael and Carol Fletcher and everyone at the Nanny Brow Country House Hotel in The Lakes. Hubert and Carol Lowry for their love and wonderful advice on Northern Ireland. Everyone at Waterton Press, especially lovely Louise who did such a great job putting this book together, thank you from your favourite chef! Garry Manning and everyone at the Manning Partnership for distributing this classical book. Susan Shaw and everyone at Carlton Studio's and The Carlton Food Network. Angela Kelly and the Bolton Evening News. Cliff Birchall and the Advertiser group of newspapers. Ian Robinson for the photograph on the jacket sleeve.

Finally, my wife Jayne, without her presence I would be nothing. Should I have forgotten anyone, it was not intentional. Thank you all. . .ENJOY.
TOM BRIDGE - International Master Chef

Cheddar, 1908.

Introduction

The Golden Age of Food is a compilation of recipes and wonderful pictures from around the British Isles and Eire. My love of the true character of food and of the facts and stories behind our heritage, will make this unique cookery book a prized possession for everyone interested in the food and drink of rural England, Ireland, Scotland and Wales.

Despite spending most of my working life in kitchens around Britain, I really never considered the power behind the food around this wonderful country. I have toured the whole area: Devon, Cornwall, Cheshire, Lancashire, The Lakes, Yorkshire and Lands End to John O' Groats, enjoying the food and drink in restaurants, pubs and Inns, the outstanding scenic views and the warm welcome from the people of Britain. Being a very keen food Historian I wanted to write The Golden Age of Food, giving you my views and a taste of old and modern Britain with a wonderful collection of panoramic sepia photographs that will make you smile.

I wrote this cookery book for the sheer pleasure of being involved in my first love, British food. This is a varied selection of my personal choice of some of the best recipes that can be found. I have tried to cover all areas and counties.

These traditional recipes from around Britain and Ireland will bring back the true heritage of the kitchens and recipes our grandmothers created. Now you can try for yourself the recipes of that golden era when food was really at its best. I have modernised some of the recipes using continental flavours like olive oils, garlic, and the produce which can now be obtained on our doorsteps every day of the week. In the golden era there was no need to advertise organic produce, the eggs for the Yorkshire pudding came from a real chicken not an ever-ready hen, the flour was milled over and over again to make it fine and the milk came from the cows that chewed the lush grass from the pastures of this wonderful land. The home-bred traditions of the British people now stretch to every table throughout the world.

Every farmhouse kitchen had hams hanging from the ceiling and the smell of new bread and oatcakes heavy in the air. . . . Oatcakes, bread and pies are still made in the old fashioned way with love, care and devotion. We have a great deal to be thankful for when it comes to our heritage. The pie chapter in this book shows the skills the cooks from that era had. I only change the timings and method to make it easier for you to use my recipes. Traditional steak and kidney, apple & pork, the beautiful marbling

Town Hall, Bolton

colours of the three layer cheese, Cheshire Pork Pies, Lancashire Hot Pot, mint pasties and venison pasty with pastry that melts in your mouth. The York Ham, Bury Black Pudding, Irish White Pudding, Yorkshire Pudding, oatcakes, Parkin & Lancashire, Irish, Cheshire, Stilton and Wensleydale cheeses are foods that are frequently seen on tables throughout the world.

The Glorious Twelfth brings game to the forefront in the cookery calendar and the chapter on game gives you grouse, duckling, partridge, pheasant, rabbit, hare and venison, a paradise for the lover of game.

Winter comes very quickly around the coast lines of Britain and recipes like King Edward's Oyster Soup, Salcombe Bay Crab Soup and Roast Sirloin of Beef with Herb Stuffing will certainly keep out the cold.

There are no regions in England more picturesque than the South Coast, the North Lakes, Yorkshire National Park and Cheshire. The final chapter is on the food that keeps the English on the map of Europe, no one can compete with our jams and preserves: home-made strawberry jam, Yorkshire Relish, rowan jelly, piccalilli and beetroot and rhubarb chutney are the accompaniments to the many dishes that bring you to the heart of this wonderful book.

Chapter 1

FAVOURITE SOUPS

Soup formed part of the dinner in the Victorian household and dinner, being the grand solid meal of the day was a matter of considerable importance.

"A well-served table is a striking index of human ingenuity and resource" said Mrs Beeton in her *All About Cookery*.
She went on to say:
"The elegance with which a dinner is served depends, of course, partly upon the means, but still more upon the taste of the master and mistress of the house. It may be observed in general, that there should always be flowers on the table, and as they form no item of expense where a garden is, there is no reason why they should not be employed every day.

The variety of the dishes which furnish forth a modern dinner-table (1860s) does not necessarily imply anything unwholesome or anything capricious. Food that is not well relished cannot be digested; and the appetite of the overworked man of business, or statesman, or of any dweller in towns, whose occupations are exciting and exhausting must suit their mode of dining to their mode of living."

If that applied in today's world the dinners would be very small. Every dinner started with some form of soup or broth. The Prince Regent loved game soup, but started his meals with caviar and finished with Rosa Lewis's famous Quail Pudding.

The great chefs and cooks of the British Isles all had one thing in common, they would never throw away the water in which meat, fish or vegetables had been boiled. This is the basis for good stock for soups and sauces. Soup has always been part of the British diet, we have to be the soup lovers of the world and with hundreds at hand I have picked the favourites from around the coastlines, towns and villages of our wonderful country.

KING EDWARD'S OYSTER SOUP

*C*alibration here with Escoffier and Rosa Lewis to create this very English soup for the then Prince of Wales becoming King Edward VII. Oysters were plentiful then and not expensive. They helped to fill out pies because meat was more costly.

— INGREDIENTS —

100g/4 oz unsalted butter

50g/2 oz plain white flour

1.4 ltr/2 pints fish stock, hot

300ml /10 fl oz cream

1 tablespoon lemon juice

salt

freshly milled white pepper

24 Fresh oysters

2 egg yolks, blended with the oyster juice

1 sprig parsley, finely chopped

— METHOD —

- To open the oysters: carefully wrap a napkin or teatowel around your (holding) hand. Place the oyster on the palm of your hand with the flat side facing upwards. Slip an oyster knife or sharp but solid (not to bend) kitchen knife under the hinge in the shell and push it into the oyster, along the top of the inside shell. Jerk up the knife and the shell will open.

- Repeat this with all the oysters. Pour the juice from the oysters into a small jug and place the oysters into a bowl, ensuring that there are no bits of shell with the oysters.

- Melt the butter in a large saucepan. Blend in the flour. Add the fish stock, stirring continuously.

- Add the cream and lemon juice. Season with salt and freshly milled black pepper.

- Strain the soup through a fine non-metallic sieve into a clean saucepan. Gently bring to the boil then remove from the heat immediately.

- Just before you serve the soup, add the oysters and then very carefully whisk in the egg yolks with the oyster juice. Sprinkle with parsley and serve immediately.

This soup is excellent during the summer served cold, topped with fresh strawberries served with a dry white wine.

COCK~A~LEEKIE SOUP

I have always said that nobody can make soups like the Scots. Baxter's tinned soups have been made for years and are known for their very fresh ingredients, which is not the case with most tinned soups. This is really a main course soup and was originally made with beef and chicken. You can also add a little rice and peppers to add colour should you wish to.

METHOD

● Melt the butter in a large saucepan and fry off the chicken and leeks for 8 minutes.

● Add the stock and bouquet garni sachet, seasoning well to taste.

● Bring the soup to the boil and simmer for 45 minutes.

● Add the prunes, with a little rice and diced peppers if you wish and simmer for 20 minutes.

● Serve with croutons or with my Irish Soda Bread *(recipe on page 174)*.

INGREDIENTS

30g/1 oz butter

350g/12 oz uncooked chicken meat, bones removed

350g/12 oz leeks, washed and cut into 2.5cm/1 inch pieces

1.1 ltrs/2 pints chicken stock

1 bouquet garni sachet

salt

freshly milled white pepper

8 prunes, stoned and halved

Ruins of Inverlocky Castle, c.1890.

CULLEN SKINK

*C*ullen is a fishing village on the Moray Firth and skink is a Scottish word meaning soup, stock or broth. This recipe dates back to Moray Firth smokeries, where oak chippings from old whisky barrels added a unique flavour to smoked finnan haddock. One recipe I created years ago was Haddock Tams Brigg for a Taste of Scotland cookery competition in Ayrshire. Yes, I did win but I was given a tankard full of the taste of Scotland and cannot remember the rest of the evening or what ever happened to the tankard!

INGREDIENTS

350g/12 oz smoked finnan haddock, skinned

600ml/1 pint milk

600ml/1 pint water

450g/1lb sliced potatoes, cooked

25g/1 oz butter

salt

freshly milled black pepper

METHOD

● Place the haddock into a large saucepan, cover with boiling water and simmer for about 6 minutes.

● Remove the bones from the fish, return them to the stock and boil for 20 minutes.

● Remove the haddock from the stock and flake.

● Strain the stock and add the milk, potatoes and the flaked fish simmer for 15 minutes, adjusting the seasoning and adding the butter and a little cream should you wish to; garnish with parsley and serve with crusty wholemeal bread.

CHEF'S ALTERNATIVE TIP

For a more luxurious flavour try this recipe with smoked salmon ends, which are far cheaper than sides of smoked salmon, topped with flakes of fresh smoked salmon, but only boil for 10 minutes instead of 20.

IRISH POTATO & PARSLEY SOUP

I was taught how to make this in Dublin by Paul Christopher several years ago. The potato has been part of the Irish diet for centuries and this recipe comes originally from Moira in County Down, Northern Ireland.

METHOD

● Fry the bacon in a large saucepan for 4 minutes, add the butter, potatoes and onion and cook for 12 minutes, stirring all the time.

● Add the stock and milk, bring to the boil and simmer for 20 minutes.

● Blend in the cream and simmer for 5 minutes, add the parsley and serve with Irish Soda bread *(recipe on page 174)*

INGREDIENTS

3 smoked streaky bacon rashers, rindless and chopped

25g/1 oz best butter

450g/1lb King Edward potatoes, chopped

450g/1lb onions, chopped

600ml/1 pint chicken stock

600ml/1 pint fresh milk

150ml/5 fl oz double cream

salt

freshly milled black pepper

freshly chopped parsley

Trinity College, Dublin, 1897.

WELSH LEEK SOUP - (CAWL CENNIN)

The flavour of this soup can be enhanced with a strong stock made from Spanish onions and about 900g/2lb of boiled lamb bones. This should be simmered for at least 4 hours. This recipe dates back to 1675 and was often served with Welsh oatcakes.

INGREDIENTS

450g/lb leeks, trimmed, sliced and washed

25g/1 oz butter

350g/12 oz onions (Spanish) chopped

2 celery sticks, chopped

1.2 ltr/2 pints lamb stock

salt

freshly milled black pepper

100ml/4 fl oz double cream

chives

Conwy Castle and Bridge, 1906.

METHOD

● Melt the butter in a large saucepan, add the leeks, onion and celery and cook gently for 10 minutes.

● Add the lamb stock and simmer for 30 minutes.

● Season to taste and add the cream. Reheat and serve with chopped chives.

CAULIFLOWER CHEESE SOUP

 r Creme du Barry, to our fellow chefs in France, taken from our classic list about 100 years ago, when Alexis Soyer started his soup kitchens during the Crimean War for dear Florence Nightingale.

METHOD

- Trim the cauliflower florets from the stalk and place them to one side.

- Cook the stalk gently in boiling salted water for 30 minutes.

- Reserve 300ml/½ pint of the cauliflower water and remove the stalk. Mash it to a pulp or put it through a blender.

- Put the butter into a saucepan and gently cook the florets for 4 minutes, remove them and place to one side.

- Blend the sifted flour into the butter and add the cauliflower water.

- Cook and stir the mixture until it thickens, slowly adding the milk. Bring to the boil, add the stalk pulp, florets and cheese and cook for 4 minutes. Pour the soup into a tureen, add the parsley cream and season with freshly milled white pepper.

Serve this soup with chunks of fresh oatmeal bread and a glass of ice cold cider.

INGREDIENTS

1 large cauliflower

50g/2 oz salted butter

25g/1 oz plain flour, sifted

300ml/½ pint fresh milk

125g/5 oz English Cheddar cheese, grated

15 ml/1 tablespoon chopped parsley

45 ml/3 tablespoons double cream

freshly milled white pepper

LONDON PARTICULAR

Winter brought a great deal of smog to London town and the Pea Soup smog, as it was known, was referred to as London Particular by Charles Dickens in his book Bleak House.

The north of England and Ireland add pig's trotters to their pea soup, in Shropshire they add mint. Years ago we had to soak the peas overnight, you can now buy them ready soaked.

— INGREDIENTS —

3 rashers smoked, rindless streaky bacon, diced

1 large onion, chopped

small knob butter

450g/1lb ready soaked peas

2.3 litres/4 pints of chicken stock

salt

freshly milled black pepper

150ml/5 fl oz double cream

chopped parsley

croutons

— CHEF'S TIP —

Some cooks strain rather than blend this soup. If you let it stand and allow the peas to dry out, they can then be blended and used to thicken vegetable soup and stews.

— METHOD —

● Put the bacon and onion into a large saucepan with a little butter and cook over a gentle heat for 6 minutes.

● Add the peas and the stock to the pan, bring to the boil, season lightly with salt and freshly milled black pepper, cover and simmer for 2 hours.

● Add the cream and blend thoroughly. Sprinkle with parsley and top with cheesy croutons.

Royal Exchange, London, c.1910.

OXTAIL SOUP WITH TARRAGON DUMPLINGS

With several tinned and pre-packed varieties of oxtail soup, the original, subtle taste is not known to most of us. The combination of fresh oxtails and tarragon dumplings is something that every lover of good British food should experience. This recipe is made in two stages, but I am sure you will find it worth the effort.

— OXTAIL SOUP METHOD —

● Chop the oxtail into pieces through its natural joints, coating lightly with seasoned flour. Quickly fry the pieces in a large, deep saucepan in the hot butter until they are lightly browned.

● Peel and dice the vegetables into 2.54cm (1 inch) squares.

● Add the oil to the pan and brown them together with the oxtail. Pour over the claret and add all the rest of the ingredients, except the beef stock.

● Cook for 10 minutes, then gradually add the beef stock. Simmer for 3 hours, skimming of any excess fat, while simmering.

● Strain off the liquid into large clean saucepan and allow it to cool.

● Remove the meat from the oxtail and chop finely. Return it to the soup, re-boil and correct the seasoning. Allow it to simmer while making the dumplings.

— TARRAGON DUMPLING METHOD —

● Mix together all the dry ingredients in a large, clean bowl.

● Add the egg and blend in thoroughly. Add enough milk to make the dough moist, shape into small balls, roll them in a little flour and cook them for about 10 minutes in boiling salted water.

● Remove them carefully and add them to the soup. Cook for a further 12 minutes.

Serve with home-made crusty bread.

— INGREDIENTS —

OXTAIL SOUP
1 whole oxtail

50g/2oz plain flour (seasoned)

100g/4oz butter

1 ½ litres/3 pints beef stock

3 tablespoons of sunflower oil

1 large carrot

1 stick celery

1 onion

small turnip

1 teaspoon thyme

1bay leaf

110/4floz Claret or sherry

salt & freshly ground black pepper

TARRAGON DUMPLINGS
50/2oz self-raising flour

50g/2oz fresh breadcrumbs

2 tablespoons shredded suet

2 tablespoons fresh tarragon leaves

2 tablespoons finely grated lemon rind

1 egg

salt & freshly ground pepper

SALCOMBE BAY CRAB SOUP

I first tasted this soup at the Anchor Inn at Star Cross, near Dawlish, and to say it was good would be an understatement, Devonshire crabs are very large and the combination of their rich meat, sherry and cream make this a soup to remember.

— INGREDIENTS —

225g/8 oz fresh crab meat

1 large onion, sliced

1.2 Litre/2 pint fish stock

50g/2 oz butter

25g/1 oz plain flour

grated rind and juice of
1 orange

275 ml/½ pint double cream

50 ml/2floz dry sherry

15 ml/1 tablespoon
anchovy essence

salt

freshly milled black pepper

— METHOD —

● Melt the butter in a large saucepan, add the onion and crab meat and cook gently for 6 minutes. Add the flour, stirring thoroughly to avoid lumps. Very slowly add the fish stock, stirring all the time until the soup comes to the boil. Allow it to simmer for 40 minutes.

● Season with salt and freshly milled black pepper, adding the anchovy essence, orange juice and rind, sherry and cream.

● Reheat and serve with brown crusty bread and a dry white wine.

The Quay, Appledore, 1923.

Eighteenth Century Green Pea Soup

*F*lorence White wrote a marvellous book called *Good Things In England* in 1929 and this recipe was in it. I have converted it to our modern weights for your use and am sure you will find it well worth the two guineas Madam Parker gave for the receipt in the eighteenth century.

At Henley-on-Thames during the regatta the soup stall sold a bowl of thick green broth for $^1/_2 d$, with a lump of bread, 3 farthings! Things are still as expensive today!

— Method —

- Melt the butter in a large saucepan, add the bacon, celery and onion. Cook for 5 minutes.

- Add the milk, stock, peas, mint and shredded lettuce and season well.

- Bring to the boil and simmer for 35 minutes.

- Sieve or strain the soup.

- Float the cucumber and cauliflower florets onto the soup and serve with warm crusty bread. Sell for at least £12.9s.3d. a pint.

— INGREDIENTS —

25g/1 oz butter

125g/4 ozs rindless smoked bacon, diced

450g/1lb ready soaked peas

600ml/1 pint of fresh milk

600ml/1 pint of beef stock

1 sprig fresh mint

2 celery sticks diced

1 cos lettuce, shredded

salt

freshly milled black pepper

1 cucumber, deseeded and diced

1 onion sliced

1 cauliflower cooked and made into florets (warm)

GAME SOUP WITH SHERRY

*T*his recipe is served in most game shooting area's of the British Isles and is very popular with the golfing fraternity, why I don't know! Maybe it has something to do with shooting a birdie!

Game can be bought today in most superstores ready cut and trimmed.

For an extra boost to this recipe add some fresh cranberry juice instead of using a full litre of beef stock on a 50/50 basis.

— INGREDIENTS —

50g/2 oz butter

1 onion, peeled and diced

1 carrot, peeled and diced

1 stick of celery, diced

450g/lb diced venison, fat removed

450g/lb any chopped game meat, (rabbit, pheasant or grouse)

50g/2 oz plain flour

1 ltr beef stock

1 bay leaf

8 black peppercorns

pinch salt

3 tablespoon redcurrant jelly

150ml/¼pint of cream sherry

— METHOD —

● Melt the butter in a saucepan, add the onions, carrot, celery and game meat, cook slowly for 6 minutes, then sprinkle with flour.

● Cook for a further 2 minutes slowly adding the stock with the bay leaf, peppercorns and salt. Simmer for 1 hour.

● Add the redcurrant jelly and sherry, let the game stock stand for at least 4 hours, remove the bay leaf and put the stock and game meat through a blender or liquidizer.

● Reheat and simmer for 10 minutes and serve with croutons.

'Rotary Kitchener' Stove

Chapter 2

SAVOURIES

*M*any people from the EEC Countries very rarely see the best of British cookery and I feel it should be revived for our overseas visitors to try. The Spanish have Tapas, the French have the Hor-d'oeuvre and the British have Savouries.

*M*y wife Jayne and I put this selection of tasty Savouries together alongside their stories and history on how they became popular. They make an excellent light lunch, supper or buffet for visiting friends.

Highgate, Kendal, 1914.

BEEF POTTED

*W*orcestershire early Eighteenth Century
Bake a tender piece of beef in butter till very tender. Drain it from the gravy, season it with cloves, mace, nutmeg, pepper and salt. Pound it in a stone mortar with a wooden beater adding fresh butter; when smooth and fine put it in your pots, close, clear the oyl'd butter from the gravey and pour over; if not enough oyle some butter and pour over.

INGREDIENTS

YORKSHIRE POTTED
BEEF, 1931.
450g/1lb rump steak, diced

½ teaspoon mace

pinch white pepper & salt

50g/2oz butter, warmed

150ml/5floz beef stock

METHOD

● Place the meat into a saucepan with half the butter, the beef stock and the salt and pepper. Simmer until tender for about 90 minutes.

● Strain the gravy into a bowl. Mince the steak very fine, adding a little gravy and the mace.

● Place into small moulds and top with the oiled butter.

Worcester Cathedral, 1923.

BLACK PUDDING COUNTRY

J have had the pleasure of meeting Andrew Holt, the owner of a business you would never think would win prizes in Europe. Well, Andrew won Gold and Silver medals at the 16th International Black Pudding competition in Belgium for the Best in Great Britain. This family run business in Rossendale, maintains exceptionally high standards. Using a recipe that dates back to 1879. (I am not going to even try to reproduce the recipe.) In restaurants throughout Great Britain the 'in' thing at the moment is Black Pudding Bread. One of my favourite recipes is Black Pudding and Potato Bake with Mustard Sauce. My mother used to make a Hot-Pot which was always lined with slices of black pudding. Andrew who now owns the business of R.S. Ireland in Waterfoot Rossendale, supplies most of the market area's and his Black Puddings can also be tasted at my favourite eatery, Northcote Manor at Langho. For something completely different try my Black Pudding Bread *(recipe on page 183).*

THE FAR FAMED BLACK PUDDING - Thornley's Pork Butchers, Chorley, 1920.

*T*AKE *groats and pearl barley, tie it up loosely in a bag and boil until cooked, place in a large tub and add seasoning, flour and onions chopped. Mix well whilst hot. Add cubes of back fat or leaf cut into quarter inch squares. Now add the blood and stiffen with oatmeal.*

*F*ILL *into a bullock runner with pudding filler, allowing about 6 to 8 pieces of fat to each pudding. Tie up firmly and boil gently for about 20 minutes. The method of Black pudding making was quite different again in 1811. I do suggest that you do not attempt to try this recipe.*

BLACK PUDDINGS - The Frugal Housewife, Manchester 1811.

*B*EFORE *you kill a hog, get a peck of groats, boil them half an hour in water, then drain them, and put them in a clean tub or large pan. Then kill your hog, save two quarts of the cold blood, and keep stirring it till it is quite cold: then mix it with your groats, and stir them well together. Season with a large teaspoon of salt, a quarter ounce of cloves, mace and nutmeg together, an equal quantity of each; dry it, beat it well and mix in.*

*T*HE *next day take the leaf (fat) of the hog, and cut it into dice, scrape, and wash the guts very clean, then tie one end and begin to fill them, but be sure to put in a good deal of fat, fill the skins three parts full, tie the other end, and make your puddings what length you please; prick them with a pin, and put them in a kettle of boiling water. Boil them slowly for an hour, then take them out and lay them on straw.*

BURY BLACK PUDDING & POTATO WITH MUSTARD SAUCE

I am not for one minute suggesting you try the old methods of black pudding making, but they are amusing to read. Very few people make their own black pudding mix, but you can now buy a black pudding making kit!

Sauce is the soul of food and I am sure you will appreciate this very novel recipe which comes from my home town of Bolton. For a more unique flavour add a taste of Ireland with some slices of white pudding.

——INGREDIENTS——

4 rings fat free, black puddings

4 large potatoes, peeled, boiled and thickly sliced

2 apples peeled, cored and sliced

2 onions, peeled and thinly sliced

50g/2oz butter

50g/2oz plain flour

100ml/3floz coarse grain mustard

1 tablespoon English mustard

300ml/9floz beef stock

a pinch nutmeg & thyme

salt

freshly ground black pepper

100g/4oz Cheddar cheese, grated

—— METHOD ——

● PRE-HEAT the oven to gas 6/400f/200c.

● Slice the black pudding 2-3 cm/1 inch in thickness, removing any skin.

● Line a deep baking dish, with the slices of potato.

● In a saucepan fry the onions in the butter. Remove the onions with a slotted spoon, retaining the butter in the pan for later. Place the onions over the potatoes, covering them completely.

● Add the slices of apple to the base of the dish covering the onions, then finish off with the black pudding.

● Put the flour and mustards into the pan in which the onions were fried and cook for 2 minutes. Slowly add the stock, stirring constantly until the sauce is smooth.

● Add the nutmeg and thyme to the sauce, taste and season with salt and pepper.

● Finally, pour the sauce over the black pudding, sprinkle with grated cheese and bake in the oven for 20 minutes.

Potted Smoked Trout

*I*n the Lakes they made this recipe with char and in Northern Ireland they use smoked mackerel, the Scots use salmon, the Welsh herrings and mackerel. This is my traditional English recipe, which I have adapted from a very old cookery book.

— Method —

- Place the fillets into a large bowl with all the ingredients except the lemon and parsley.

- Pound the mixture until it is very smooth or place it into a blender or liquidizer.

- Place the smoked trout mixture into one large buttered or individual buttered earthenware pots.

- Cover with buttered greaseproof paper and weigh them down with something heavy.

- Place into the refrigerator for at least 4 hours.

- Remove the paper and dress the trout with slices of fresh lemon and parsley.

Serve the smoked trout with slices of warm toast.

— INGREDIENTS —

8 fillets smoked trout
(skinned & de-boned)

a generous pinch of nutmeg & mace

100g/4oz softened butter

salt

freshly milled black pepper

30ml/2 tablespoon port or sherry

30ml/2 tablespoon double cream

1 lemon thinly sliced

freshly washed sprigs of parsley

25g/1oz butter for the earthenware pots

MORECAMBE BAY POTTED SHRIMPS

*T*he best shrimps to use for this recipe are the small brown shrimps, these can be purchased from any quality fishmonger.

Morecambe Bay have been producing these for hundreds of years, they became very popular during the Victorian period when visitors from all over England came for their traditional Easter and Summer breaks. A quick and simple recipe, it is very important that you do not boil the shrimps but gently and slowly heat them. I created a simple dish using pre-baked mini tartlets and smoked Kinsale oysters. Place 2 tablespoons of the shrimps, butter, nutmeg and seasoning into each tartlet, warm slowly in the oven and garnish with smoked oysters and lemon.

— INGREDIENTS —

450g/1lb Morecambe bay shrimps

225g/8 oz softened butter

generous pinch nutmeg, cayenne pepper

salt and freshly milled black pepper.

1 lemon cut into wedges

— METHOD —

● Place all the ingredients into a pan and heat them gently. (DO NOT BOIL) Stir the shrimps very carefully until they are well coated with butter.

● Place the shrimps into individual ramekins or one small potting dish and cover with butter.

● Allow them to cool for 2 hours and serve with thinly sliced buttered brown bread or warm toast, with a wedge of fresh lemon.

Southport Shrimpers.

CHESHIRE POTTED CHEESE

*B*eing a great cheese lover, I can really relate to this type of recipe which is very rarely seen on the lunch table today! Stilton is potted quite regularly and is available at most superstores but it was Richard Dolby, cook at the Thatched House Tavern in St James's Street, London that served his recipe to the customers with a jug of porter. Potted Cheshire Cheese was introduced around 1700 and it was Hannah Glasse who in the 1740's produced her version in the *Art of Cookery*.
This original cheese recipe is now served in earthenware jars at Fortnum & Mason's and Harrods in London.

— *TO POT CHESHIRE CHEESE* —

● Take three pounds of Cheshire Cheese, and put it into a mortar with half a pound of the best fresh butter you can get.

● Pound them together, and in the beating add a gill of rich Canary Wine and half an ounce of Mace finely beat, then sifted to a fine powder.

● When all is extremely well mixed, press it hard down in a gallipot. Cover it with clarified butter, and keep it cool.

"A slice of this exceeds all the Cream Cheese that can be made".
Hannah Glasse 1740.

Top - St. Mary's Church, Chester, 1906.
Right - Bollands Restaurant, Chester.

AUTHORS RECIPE - POTTED STILTON

— INGREDIENTS —

450g/1lb mellow Stilton

100g/4 oz unsalted butter, softened

generous pinch powdered mace

1 teaspoon of English mustard

2 tablespoons Port

100g/4oz clarified butter

— METHOD —

● Mash all the ingredients together thoroughly, or mix in a blender until texture becomes very creamy.

● Place the blended Stilton into earthenware or ramekin dishes, ensuring that the cheese is pressed down firmly.

● Top with clarified butter and place into the refrigerator for at least 2 days.

Serve with my fresh *Eccles Cakes, (recipe page 155)* toast or fresh bread.

— CLARIFIED BUTTER —

● Place 225g/8oz fresh unsalted butter, into a saucepan and heat very slowly, skimming off the foam as the butter heats up.

● The sediment will sink to the bottom of the pan as the butter heats.

● When the butter has completely melted, remove the pan from the heat and leave it to stand for 2 minutes allowing the sediment to sink to the bottom.

● Very slowly and carefully pour the clarified butter into a small container, leaving the sediment in the pan. The butter is then ready for use in pouring over the surface of your potted dishes.

Wiltshire Cheese & Ham Bites

Wiltshire was once known as pig country, every small holding had pigs, they were looked after by the whole household, growing fat on scraps of potato and greens grown on the plots, then come Christmas it was goodbye Porky, it's time for some ham!

This recipe is a very novel way of using up ends of cheese, ham, chicken, bacon, etc. It is one of those that everyone had to use during the war, it was *fill yer up before ya gata work,* that's if you had work!

— Method —

- In a saucepan bring the butter and water to the boil and remove from the heat. Add the flour stirring briskly until the mixture forms a soft ball, cool slightly.

- Slowly add the eggs, beating them until the mixture becomes smooth.

- Add the rest of the ingredients, mixing well.

- Drop small teaspoons of the mixture into the hot fat, frying each one for 4 minutes at a time, until they are golden brown.

- You can use your favourite cheese with this recipe, one I really enjoy is Stilton with grated Pear, served with a glass of Port.

— Chef's Alternative Tip —
For a vegetarian version you can use shredded vegetables in place of the meat

— INGREDIENTS —

50g/2oz butter or marg

120ml/8 tablespoons water

100g/4oz flour

4 eggs

50g/2oz Cheddar cheese, grated

50g/2oz York ham or cooked chicken, chopped

1 small, finely chopped onion

salt

freshly milled black pepper

cooking oil or dripping for deep frying

Scotch Woodcock

his recipe was first introduced in the second quarter of the nineteenth century, and certainly represents the quality of English cookery during this period.

— INGREDIENTS —

4 slices medium or thick bread

50g/2oz soft butter

8 Anchovies

4 eggs

150ml/5 floz double cream

Ground black pepper and salt

The Shambles, York, c.1955.

— METHOD —

● Toast the bread, and butter well on both sides.

● After washing and scraping the anchovies spread them between the two slices of toast.

● Beat the yolks of the eggs with the cream and season well, (a small pinch of cayenne may also be used). Pour the liquid slowly into a saucepan and gently heat, taking care to only thicken but not to boil. Remove the saucepan from the heat.

● Pour the sauce over the pieces of buttered toast, criss-cross with anchovies and serve immediately.

● For the more health conscious fromage frais may be used for a lighter texture.

Caviare being very expensive in the early eighteenth century, this recipe for 'Mock Caviare' appeared from a Dr Hunter from York in 1806.

'Take anchovies, parsley and chives or shallots.
Pound them in a marble mortar, with some olive-oil, salt and lemon juice.
Make a toast of white bread and spread the mixture upon it.
Cut it into neat pieces and serve it up'.

He then goes onto say: *'This is a very good substitute for Caviare'.*

A Delicious Savoury From Northern Ireland

I used to make this for a hotel near Whipsnade several years ago. I made a rich cheese sauce, chopped up grilled Cumberland sausage, with crispy Irish bacon, a little mashed potato and freshly chopped parsley. So well before quiches became a fashion, we had our Northern Irish idea of what a quiche would look like rolled up, so in the 1900's we came up with this wonderful idea, then the French came along and flattened it! Frogs who'd eat them!

Elizabeth Raffald the most famous Northern cook wrote her own version for a Savoury in her cookery book in 1769, which I believe to be the first Cheese Toastie.

"To Make a Nice Whet before Dinner

1. Cut some slices of bread half an inch thick.

2. Fry them in butter, but not too hard.

3. Then split some anchovies, take out the bones, and lay half an anchovy on each piece of bread.

4. Have ready some Cheshire cheese grated, and some chopped parsley mixed together.

5. Lay it pretty thick over the bread and anchovy.

6. Baste it with butter.

7. Brown it with a salamander (grill that held bread like a toasting fork)

8. It must be done on the dish in which you send it to the table."

Elizabeth Raffald 1733-1781
The Experienced English Housekeeper, for the use and ease of Ladies, Housekeepers and Cooks.

Albert Memorial & Corn Market, Belfast, 1897.

NORTHERN IRISH SAVOURY

— INGREDIENTS —

225g/8oz self raising flour

1 teaspoon baking powder

a pinch of salt

100g/4oz shredded suet

water

25g/1oz beef dripping

3 onions, peeled and sliced

8 rashers smoked rindless
middle bacon

175g/6oz Irish Cheddar cheese

100g/4oz cooked mashed
potato

1 egg blended with 2
tablespoons double cream

salt

freshly milled black pepper

1 teaspoon chopped sage

1 egg, beaten for glaze

— METHOD —

- PRE-HEAT the oven to gas 5/375f/190c.

- Sift the flour, baking powder and salt into a large mixing bowl, blend in the suet and slowly add sufficient water to make a stiff dough.

- Flour and roll out the dough to an oblong 30 x 15cm (12 x 6 inch).

- Heat the dripping and fry the onions and bacon until cooked (approx 6 minutes). Allow the bacon to cool and then chop roughly.

- Place the bacon and onion into a clean bowl, adding the cheese, potato, egg, cream, salt and freshly milled black pepper. Blend the mixture well until it is creamy but firm.

- Put the mixture onto the pastry, sprinkle with sage.

- Brush the sides of the mixture with beaten egg and roll the pastry up (swiss roll style), sealing the ends.

- Make 3 diagonal cuts into the top of the pastry and place on a lightly greased baking sheet.

- Place into the centre of the oven and bake for 50 to 60 minutes until golden brown.

- Slice when it is just warm and serve with a pot of English tea.

SUSSEX FRITTERS

*S*ussex Fritters were originally served at Cowdray Park near Midhurst in beautiful Sussex in the early eighteenth century. Try using minced cornbeef or left over lamb, should you not have any ham. It's a recipe you can really utilise anything with.

— METHOD —

● Mash the warm potatoes with the butter, gently blend in the ham and parsley, seasoning well.

● Beat an egg and add to the mixture. Shape the mixture into small balls.

● Beat the 2nd egg well with 2 tablespoons of milk and place it into a large saucer.

● Put the breadcrumbs on a plate and then coat the balls of mixture with the egg roll through the breadcrumbs and fry.

Serve with a light egg salad.

— INGREDIENTS —

225g/8oz cooked potatoes, warm

50g/2oz softened butter

110g/4oz cooked York ham, finely minced

1 tablespoon finely chopped parsley

Freshly ground black pepper

salt

2 eggs

50g/2oz freshly toasted brown breadcrumbs

North Street, Midhurst, 1921.

NORWICH CREAMED VEAL KIDNEYS

*N*orwich is the home of Colman's mustard shop in Bridewell Alley and this was one of the very first recipes to be served to Horatio Nelson. One of the most beautiful sites when you approach Norwich is the magnificent Cathedral.

— INGREDIENTS —

75g/3oz butter

8 veal kidneys, trimmed and sliced thinly

175g/6oz button mushrooms, sliced

1 teaspoon Colman's mustard

pinch freshly minced ginger

salt

freshly milled black pepper

2 tablespoon dry sherry

150ml/5floz double cream

4 slices hot toast cut into triangles

sprigs fresh parsley

— METHOD —

● Pre-heat the oven gas 5, 375f/190c.

● Melt the butter in a large saucepan and gently fry the kidneys for 4 minutes. Remove the kidneys with a slotted spoon place in a serving dish and keep warm. Add the mushrooms to the frying pan, cooking them in the leftover juices, add the mustard, ginger, salt and freshly milled black pepper.

● Cook for 2 minutes then add the sherry and cream, Cook for a further 3 minutes, then pour over the kidneys. Bake in the oven for 10 minutes.

● Place triangles of warm toast around the kidneys , with sprigs of fresh parsley and serve, with one arm tucked into your blouse or shirt! . . . .

TOAD-IN-THE-HOLE

*T*oad-in-the-hole today is like a national institution. Years ago beef, chicken, goat and even fish were used, not the great British banger. My preference is Cumberland sausage but you can try this recipe using other cooked meats should you like to.

It is far better to make the batter the day before and let it settle.

METHOD

● PRE-HEAT the oven to gas 7/425f/220c.

● Place the pricked sausages in a deep baking tray with the dripping and bake for 10 minutes.

● Meanwhile make the batter: mix the flour and a pinch of salt in a bowl, then make a well in the centre and break in the egg.

● Add half the milk and, using a wooden spoon, work into the flour to form a paste, beating the mixture until it is smooth. Slowly add the rest of the milk and then the water, beating until it is a smooth consistency.

● Remove the HOT tray from the oven, pour the batter over the sausages and return the tray to the oven for 20 to 30 minutes until the batter is risen and golden brown.

Serve with a rich onion gravy or a light potato salad.

INGREDIENTS

450g/1lb fresh Cumberland sausage, cut into 5cm/2inch pieces

25g/1oz beef dripping

YORKSHIRE PUDDING BATTER
100g/4oz plain flour
pinch of salt

1 large fresh egg

200ml/7 floz fresh milk

100ml/3 floz cold water

CHEF'S ALTERNATIVE TIP

Add 1 tablespoon of caster sugar to the batter. Place 4 pears peeled, cored and halved onto a tray with 25g/1oz butter, using the same method.

OTHER USES FOR YORKSHIRE PUDDING BATTER - PANCAKES

I thought you might be quite amused to read the following recipe from my cookery book collection:

THE COOK & HOUSEKEEPERS DICTIONARY 1823
PANCAKES: Make a light batter of eggs, flour and milk. Fry it in a small pan, in hot dripping or lard. Salt, nutmeg or ginger may be added. Sugar and lemon should be served to eat with them. When eggs are very scarce, the batter may be made of flour and small beer, with the addition of a little ginger; or clean snow with flour and a very little milk, will serve instead of an egg!

MARY KETTILBY, 1728, AND ANN PECKHAM FROM LEEDS, 1700, USED THIS RECIPE FOR QUIRE PAPER OR THIN CREAM PANCAKES.
Take to a Pint of Cream, eight eggs, leaving out two whites, three spoonfuls of fine flour, three spoonfuls of sack (sherry) and one spoonful of orange flower water, a little sugar, a grated nutmeg and a quart of a pound of butter, melted in the cream.
Mingle all well together, mixing the flour with a little cream at first, that it may be smooth. Butter your pan for the first pan-cake, and let them run as thin as you can possibly to be whole. When one side is colour'd tis enough. Take them carefully out of the pan and strew some fine sifted sugar between each; lay them as even on each other as you can. This quantity will make twenty.

Robin Hood's Bay, Yorkshire.

Authors Revised Quire of Paper

 have revised the above for modern use. I use fresh strawberries, tossed in castor sugar and a little Drambuie and a double thick cream for the fillings for these pancakes.

— Method —

- Sieve the flour and sugar into a large clean bowl.

- Beat together the eggs, yolks, milk and cream. Pour the mixture onto the flour whisking briskly until you have a very smooth batter. Then add the sherry whisking briskly again.

- Let the batter settle for 30 minutes, then whisk briskly again before using.

- Heat a heavy non-stick omelette or pancake pan, brush generously with melted butter and fry the pancakes in the normal way.

- Make approx 8 to 10 pancakes and create your own filling using, fruit, redcurrant jelly, jam or ice-cream with butterscotch, grated chocolate, puree of apple and cinnamon, crepe's Suzette, honey, lemon and sugar or even fruit yoghurt.

— INGREDIENTS —

100g/4oz plain flour

25g/1oz castor sugar

2 eggs with 2 extra egg yolks

150ml/5 floz fresh milk

150ml/5 floz single cream

4 tablespoons sherry

butter for frying

Aldborough, Yorkshire, 1907.

GLAMORGAN SAUSAGES

his cheese flavoured savoury Glamorgan sausage (Selsigen Morgannwg) takes its name from the shape of the food.

— INGREDIENTS —

150g/5oz fresh white breadcrumbs

75g/3oz grated Cheshire cheese

1 egg separated

plain flour

75g/3oz crisp breadcrumbs for frying

oil for shallow frying

pinch mixed herbs

teaspoon mustard

a little finely chopped onion

Ground black pepper and salt

— METHOD —

● Mix together the herbs, mustard, breadcrumbs and cheese and season well.

● Bind all the above with the yolk of an egg

● Divide into small sausage shapes and roll in the flour, dip each sausage into the white of the egg and roll in breadcrumbs.

● Fry the sausages in the hot oil for 5 minutes until they are golden brown.

This can be served either hot with potatoes or cold with a fresh green salad.

— CHEF'S TIP —
You can add any of your favourite grated cheeses mix with a tablespoon of Branston pickle, or with your favourite minced cooked meat if you are not a vegetarian.

Caws Pobi - Welsh Rarebit

ne of my favourite authors is Elizabeth David and she wrote the following letter to a newspaper in 1995:

"WELSH WELSH RABBIT
Glynn Christian states that he has found no recipes for Welsh rabbit/rarebit which suggest Welsh cheese. If he were to refer to Lady Llanover's *Good Cookery*, published in 1867, he would find an authentic recipe, as follows:

'Cut a slice of the real Welsh cheese made of sheep and cow's milk, toast it at the fire on both sides, but not so much as to drop; toast a piece of bread, less than a quarter of an inch thick, to be quite crisp, and spread it very thinly with fresh cold butter on one side (it must not be saturated with butter), then lay the toasted cheese upon the bread and serve immediately on a very hot plate; the butter can, of course, be omitted.'

Lady Llanover's husband, formerly Sir Benjamin Hall, was MP for Newport in South Wales. The story goes that Big Ben was named after him."
Elizabeth David, London SW3.

— Method —

● Put the cheese, butter, Worcestershire sauce, mustard and flour into a saucepan, stirring well add the stout and ground black pepper, cook and stir continuously over a very gentle heat until smooth.

● Place onto the untoasted side of the bread very *Caerphilly* and brown under the grill.

— INGREDIENTS —

225g/8oz Gloucester, Caerphilly or Cheshire cheese, grated

25g/1oz butter

1 tablespoon Worcestershire sauce

1 teaspoon dry English mustard

1 teaspoon flour

4 tablespoons stout

freshly ground black pepper

4 slices toasted bread (one side only)

BIRMINGHAM BACON CAKES

great deal of nice food like Bourneville chocolate comes from this area of the country. Brummy cakes where served at the country fairs in late Victorian times.

— INGREDIENTS —

100g/4oz rindless streaky bacon

225g/8oz self- raising flour

25g/1oz butter

75g/3oz Cheddar cheese grated

150 ml/5 floz milk

1 tablespoon tomato ketchup

1 teaspoon Worcestershire sauce

1 tablespoon milk for glazing

watercress for garnish

salt and ground black pepper

— METHOD —

● Grill the bacon until crisp and cut into small pieces.

● Sieve flour and salt together, add butter and rub in finely.

● Add the bacon and one third of the cheese.

● Mix together milk, ketchup and Worcester sauce and add to dry ingredients to make a soft dough

● On a floured board roll out dough into a 7 in (18cm) circle

● Brush with milk and cut into 8 wedges

● Arrange on a greased baking sheet and sprinkle with the remaining cheese and bake in the centre of the oven for 20 minutes.

MARINATED MANX KIPPER FILLETS

The Isle of Man is famous for its oak-smoked kipper fillets, its TT races and an excellent racing driver by the name of Nigel, who really does favour this recipe with crushed cloves of garlic and a little cayenne pepper sprinkled on.

Other masters of the kipper trade are the curers at Loch Fyne in Scotland, but did you know that the first kippers were prepared at the Seahouses in Northumberland in the 1840s?

— METHOD —

● Cut each kipper fillet diagonally into 5 strips, following its natural grain.

● Put the rest of the ingredients into a clean bowl and blend with a wooden spoon.

● Place the fillets into this marinade and refrigerate for 12 hours.

● Place the fillets onto a serving dish garnished with lemon and parsley. Serve with rye bread and a fresh Watercress salad.

— INGREDIENTS —

3 pairs (6) uncooked, oak - smoked manx kipper fillets

MARINADE
1 teaspoon dry English mustard

1 clove of garlic crushed

3 tablespoons ground nut oil

1 tablespoon tarragon vinegar

2 shallots, finely sliced

1 tablespoon freshly chopped parsley

juice of 1 lemon

freshly milled black pepper

1 lemon sliced

2 sprigs parsley

From one giddy "KIPPER" to another

SOLOMONGUNDY (SALLID MAGUNDI)

*T*his originates from the Tudor times, I have about 14 different recipes with three different ways of spelling the dish.

I have devised a modern version of this recipe but I thought you might like to see another version so I have given here the original Mrs Glasse's " Salmagundy" from 1747.

'1. Take 2 pickled herrings and bone them; a handful of parsley, four eggs boiled hard, the meat of one roasted chicken or fowl.

2. Chop all very fine separately, that is the yolks of eggs by themselves, and the whites the same.

3. Scrape some lean boiled ham and hung beef very fine.

4. Turn a small china basin or deep saucer upside down in your dish.

5. Make some butter into the shape of a pineapple, or any other shape you please, and set on the top of the basin or saucer.

6. Lay round the basin a ring of shred parsley, then white of eggs, then ham, then chicken, then beef, then yolks of eggs, then herrings, till you have covered the basin and used all your ingredients.

7. Garnish the dish with whole capers and pickles of any sort you choose, chopped fine.

8. Or you may leave out the butter and put the ingredients in the basin and put a flower of any sort at the top, or a sprig of myrtle.'

Staple Inn & Old Houses, c.1886.

AUTHORS RECIPE - SOLOMONGUNDY

*T*his is an excellent recipe for a barbecue party or that special evening when you want to serve something extra, but you don't know what!

— METHOD —

● Cover a large oval flat platter completely with lettuce. Then, starting with the herrings, line the platter, lengthways from the top using the herrings, chicken, eggs and meats. Covering the platter completely, then line between each item of food with the mangetout, sliced grapes, olives, shallots, almonds and sultanas.

● Finally garnish with a sprinkling of orange zest, slices of orange and mint leaves. Season well with salt and freshly milled black pepper.

● Finally, pour the juice over the herrings and serve with fresh crusty bread.

— CHEF'S ALTERNATIVE TIP —

Should you wish, garnish with cold, cooked vegetables like sliced beans, baby sweetcorn and beetroot, it always looks good with red cabbage.

— INGREDIENTS —

1 large flat lettuce

8 Rollmop herrings and juice

4 x 150g/6oz chicken breast, cooked and thinly sliced

6 hard-boiled eggs, quartered

100g/4oz sliced York ham

100g/4oz sliced roast beef

100g/4oz sliced roast lamb

150g/6oz mangetout, cooked and cooled

100g/4oz seedless black grapes,

20 stuffed olives, sliced

12 shallots, peeled and boiled

50g/2oz flaked almonds

50g/2oz sultanas

sprig fresh mint leaves

2 oranges, zested and sliced

salt & freshly milled black pepper

EGGS & OMELETTES

I do remember the little lion that was stamped on eggs in the 1960s when Edwina Curry and her dear friend Salmonella was not very well known to this country.

Eggs have been popular since the beginning of time, my all time favourite breakfast when I can afford it is Smoked scotch salmon with scrambled eggs. Mrs Beeton in 1861 gave us - ALPINE EGGS :

'Butter a small fireproof dish thickly and line it with the greater part of 6 oz cheese cut into slices. Break over four eggs without breaking the yolks; seasoning them with salt and pepper. Grate the remainder of the cheese and mix it with a little chopped parsley. Lay it over the top and over this put some butter in small pieces, Bake it in a quick oven for 10 minutes and serve it hot.'
The Book of Household Management by Mrs Beeton 1861.

A FRICASSEY OF EGG - Mrs Glasse. 1747
"Boil eight eggs hard, Take off the shells, cut them into quarters, have ready half pint of Cream, and a quarter of a pound of fresh Butter, stir it together over the Fire till it is thick and smooth, lay the eggs in your dish and pour the same over. Garnish with the hard yolks of three eggs cut in two and lay around the edge of the dish"
The Art of Cookery made plain and Easy, 1747.

Crummock Water from Loweswater, 1899.

SCOTCH EGGS

*B*elieve it or not this used to be part of the Scots breakfast, along with other delights like porridge with whisky and bacon fried eggs with sliced, fried haggis. Today we serve scotch eggs with a little mustard and they make an excellent quick lunch or supper snack.

Try Cumberland or Lincolnshire sausage meat instead of pork for a more robust savoury flavour.

— METHOD —

- Roll the eggs in the seasoned flour.

- Place the sausage meat into a bowl with the parsley, shallots, nutmeg, marjoram, basil, salt and freshly milled black pepper. Work all the ingredients in together.

- Divide the sausage meat into six equal portions, flatten the meat into six rounds, placing one egg onto each round.

- Work the meat around each egg, with wet hands to form a smooth, even layer, ensuring that you seal the meat well.

- Roll each egg into the egg wash, then the breadcrumbs.

- Heat the oil and deep fry the coated eggs for 6 minutes until they are golden brown. Turn them every minute so that they cook evenly.

- Remove the Scotch eggs with a slotted spoon and place onto some kitchen paper, to remove the excess oil.

Allow them to cool and serve them, with a sweetcorn salad.

— INGREDIENTS —

6 medium size eggs, hard-boiled and shelled

seasoned flour

350g/12oz Cumberland sausage meat

1 tablespoon chopped parsley

2 shallots, finely chopped

a little grated nutmeg

pinch marjoram and basil

salt & freshly milled black pepper

1 egg, beaten with a little milk

100g/4oz freshly toasted breadcrumbs

SCOTCH SMOKED SALMON & SCRAMBLED EGGS

*O*nly the best Scotch or Irish smoked salmon should be used for this recipe and it should not be cooked with the scrambled egg, using that method only ruins the flavour of the smoked salmon. The rich and famous today still demand this as a savoury starter during a Sunday Brunch, served with a glass of Bucks Fizz.

— INGREDIENTS —

225g/8oz Scotch smoked salmon, seasoned with black pepper

8 fresh eggs

5 tablespoons double cream

salt

generous pinch freshly grated nutmeg

freshly ground black pepper

50g/2oz butter

— METHOD —

● Cut the sliced and seasoned smoked salmon into diamond shapes.

● In a large bowl mix together the eggs, cream, salt, nutmeg and pepper, whisking them well.

● Melt the butter slowly in a large non-stick frying pan, add the egg mixture and stir all the time, using a wooden spoon until the mixture becomes creamy and is just thickening, but is still wet.

● Divide the scrambled egg onto warm plates and top with diamonds of smoked salmon.

VARIATIONS ON SCRAMBLED EGGS FROM 1914
1. *Mix in anchovy essence*
2. *Add a little grated cheese*
3. *Add fresh green peas*
4. *Add some minced York ham*
5. *Blend in some diced sheep's kidney (cooked)*
6. *Blend in some diced mushrooms*
7. *Serve them onto a bed of warm spinach*
8. *Serve them onto a bed of warm tomatoes*
9. *Alternative to smoked salmon, serve with hot smoked finnan*

OMELETTES OR PAN FRIED EGGS

*W*ere mentioned in one of the very first cookery books *The Forme of Cury*, circa 1385,
which was compiled by the master cooks of Richard II.
I sincerely believe that from several writings the *AMULET* was discovered in England and not in France.

"TAKE some Egges and beat them well with a little faire water and salt, then take a frying pan and melt your Butter: and then put in your Egges, then take a knife and lift up your Egges, that the raw may goe all to the bottom of the pan, then turne it up with your knife on every side that it may become square, then lay a dish upon the pan, and then turne the pan upside down upon the dish and so serue in your Egges with Veriuyce and Vinegar, which you will."
The Forme of Cury, 1385.

I am sure you can see that this is an omelette sprinkled with verjuice or vinegar. VERJUICE is mentioned frequently in old cookery books, it is a form of di-stilled apple juice, which today they call cider vinegar.

BAKED OMELET: Florence White, 1924.

Butter a small pie dish, Beat 2 new-laid eggs with 1 tablespoon of milk, a little salt and pepper.
Pour into the dish, and bake in a moderate oven (gas 4, 350f/180c) until set.
Time five to ten minutes according to heat of oven.

AMULET OF ASPARAGUS, 1806.

Beat up six eggs with cream, boil some of the large and finest asparagus.
When boiled, cut off all the green in small pieces.
Mix them with the eggs and put in some pepper and salt.
Make a slice of butter hot in the pan, put them in, and serve them on buttered toast.

Sheep going to market, Walsingham, 1929.

THE PERFECT CHESHIRE CHEESE OMELETTE

he French make their omelettes flat, we like ours to rise and the easiest and lightest way of making an omelette is by using my method.

— INGREDIENTS —

3 eggs separated into
clean bowls

4 tablespoons double cream

salt

freshly milled black pepper

25g/1oz Cheshire cheese,
grated

25g/1oz butter

sprig fresh parsley

1 tomato, sliced

— METHOD —

● Beat the egg yolks with 2 tablespoons of cream and season, whisk the egg whites until peaky and fold into the egg yolks gently, add half the grated cheese.

● Turn on the grill to a high.

● Melt the butter in a small omelette pan, making sure the bottom and sides of the pan are coated with the butter and the pan is hot. Add the mixture and when the omelette is nearly firm but still slightly wet, add the rest of the cream and cheese. Brown quickly under the grill until the omelette rises and slide onto a warm plate and garnish with a little parsley and sliced tomato.

● This method is for a soufflé omelette, if you want a flat omelette simply do not separate the eggs and do not place under a hot grill.

EGGY BREAD

*E*very child throughout Great Britain must have tasted this at least once. I adore this recipe because any and every type of flavour could be added to the bread; if you used bacon fat and half butter to fry the bread, the flavour of bacon comes through and it is superb. Make sure the grill is on before you start this recipe.

— METHOD —

- Beat the milk and eggs together, season well with salt and freshly milled black pepper.

- Make the bread and cheese up into sandwiches and cut into triangles.

- Dip them all into the egg mixture and let them soak for a few minutes.

- Melt the butter and bacon fat in a frying pan and fry the bread on both sides until brown.

- Place them briefly under the grill and serve.

— INGREDIENTS —

150ml/5floz milk

4 fresh eggs

salt

freshly milled black pepper

8 slices white bread, buttered

100g/4oz Red Leicester cheese, grated

25g/1oz butter

25g/1oz bacon fat

— CHEF'S TIP —

Try this recipe with crispy bacon finally chopped with the grated cheese. Also try your favourite fillings, like prawns or sausage. This recipe is there to be enjoyed!

Children playing on swing.

Shrimp Toast from Lowestoft, 1870

evised by a great old chef's grandfather, Eric Shaw, who lived in Lowestoft and passed this onto his son also called Eric, who taught me to cook when I was 13 years old.

INGREDIENTS

225g/8oz brown shrimps

25g/1oz unsalted butter

1 egg, beaten with
1 tablespoon of cream

salt

pinch cayenne

8 slices toasted brown bread

anchovy paste

METHOD

● Put the shrimps with the butter into a saucepan and heat gently, when hot add the egg with cream, stirring until nearly cooked, season well with salt and cayenne pepper

● Spread the anchovy paste onto the hot toast and top with the shrimp mixture cut into triangles.

London Road, Lowestoft, 1896.

Chapter 3

FISH & SEAFOOD

I do believe that fish and chips started on the Yorkshire & Lancashire borders, and that seafood bars first opened in Brighton. Colchester is the home of the Oyster bar and eel and mash is without doubt a London delicacy. You will find some of my recipes very healthy and quite modern and I am sure you will recognise many from around the coasts, like the Fermanagh Wild Trout with smoked bacon, Cleddau Salmon and Haddock Fish Cakes and Cornish Buttered Lobster to name but a few.

Herring Barrel Making.

MEDLEY OF SEAFOOD - ON A BED OF ROSE PETAL CREAM SAUCE

*Y*ou can use almost any sea fish in my Medley of Seafood recipe. I always try to use red sea bream. When choosing fish always check the gills and the eyes of the fish for freshness. The eyes should be bright and stand out, not be flat, dull or sunken. The gills should be moist and of a red colour, not grey, the body firm to the touch not slimy. On a good fish there would almost be no smell at all, if there is it should be very 'fresh' and not stale.

— INGREDIENTS —

12 scallops

12 tiger prawns

12 crevettes

450g/1lb fillet of bream

125g/4oz fresh water prawns

50g/2oz butter

juice and zest of 1 lemon

FOR THE SAUCE
150ml/¼ pint rose petal vinegar

150ml/¼ pint of quality
white wine

pink peppercorns

saffron

salt and freshly milled black
pepper

150ml/¼ pint double cream or
fromage frais

Scotch Fisher Girls, Scarborough.

— METHOD —

● Place the vegetables in 1 litre of water, with a bay leaf and bouquet garni, simmer for 1 hour to make the vegetable stock, strain and place to one side.

● Fillet the red sea bream, cut into slices and place to one side.

● Place the crevettes onto their sides and cut down the spine with a sharp knife.

● Melt the butter in a large sauce pan and add the fish, cooking for about 1 to 2 minutes, season with ground black pepper. Add the lemon juice and zest.

● Very carefully add a pinch of saffron powder or a few strands to the juice and butter in the pan (not the fish).

● Remove the pan from the heat and place the seafood into layers onto a warm plate, place into the oven to keep warm.

● Return the pan with the juices back to the heat, add the vegetable stock, bring to the boil and reduce by $1/3$rd.

● Add the rose petal vinegar and let it reduce for 4 minutes.

● Add the peppercorns, lemon juice, white wine and turned carrots letting, it reduce for a further 6 minutes.

● Pour over the cream and simmer for 2 minutes.

● Remove the fish from the oven and lightly mask the fish with the sauce, placing the carrots around the plate.

● Should you be serving this as a main course, mash the vegetables left from the stock with some potatoes and make them into little patty shapes. Coat them with egg and breadcrumbs and shallow fry them in a little melted butter or cooking oil.

— INGREDIENTS —

VEGETABLE STOCK
1 diced carrot

1 diced onion

1 stick of celery diced

1 chopped leek

1 bay leaf

Bouquet garni

15ml/1tablespoon fresh herbs

1 clove of garlic

— CHEF'S ALTERNATIVE TIP —

*For a healthier alternative use low fat margarine instead of butter.
The fish and lemon make this a very healthy recipe.*

SALMON & SPINACH ROLL

nother of my healthy idea's, gathered in Scotland while working in Ayrshire during a Robbie Burns night, perhaps I should have called it Tams Brig on Salmon!

— INGREDIENTS —

225g/8oz cooked spinach
(drained weight)

100g/4oz fresh salmon
(poached in fish stock)

15ml/1tablespoon low-fat
margarine

15ml/1tablespoon corn oil

15g/¹/₂oz plain flour

3 eggs, separated

150ml/¹/₄ pint semi-skimmed
milk (hot)

75g/3oz button mushrooms,
thinly sliced

25g/1oz grated Parmesan
cheese

lo-salt

freshly milled black pepper

15ml/1tablespoon freshly
chopped tarragon

lemon juice and zest

— METHOD —

● PRE-HEAT the oven to gas 6/400f/200c.

● Poach the salmon in a little fish stock for 4 minutes until just cooked, then drain and chop finely.

● Grease a 8inch x 12inch swiss roll tin with the margarine.

● Into a clean bowl place the spinach and egg yolks, season them well and beat them together.

● In another bowl, whisk the egg whites until they are peaky and stiff.

● Fold the mixture in with the spinach. Place the mixture into the baking tin and sprinkle with the parmesan.

● Bake in the oven for at least 12 minutes until it is well risen and firm.

● While the Roll mix is cooking, in a saucepan heat the corn oil and cook the mushrooms for two minutes.

● Stir in the flour and slowly add the hot milk, cook for 1 minute then add the chopped salmon and fresh tarragon, beating thoroughly until it is completely blended.

● Lay out a large sheet of greaseproof paper. Spread the roll mix onto the sheet of greaseproof paper into a square shape.

● Spread over the top the salmon filling and roll it up very carefully, like you would a swiss roll.

● Seal it, rewrap in cooking foil and cook in the oven for a further 12 minutes.

Serve hot with fresh lemon juice or cold with a salad garnished with fresh tarragon leaves.

TROMPETTO'S OYSTERS

romps was my mentor and dear friend, not only a famous Savoy chef, it is not surprising that I created this recipe in 1982 from my *Golden Age of Cookery book* as a tribute.

METHOD

- PRE-HEAT oven to gas 6/400f/200c.

- In a large sauté pan, poach the oysters in their own juice for 4 minutes.

- Strain the juice into another saucepan.

- Melt the butter in a saucepan and add the flour. Cook for 2 minutes, blending all the time.

- Add the white wine and shallots, bring to the boil and add the oyster juice.

- Let it reduce by ⅓, about 1 hour.

- Add the parsley and anchovy essence, seasoning well and cook for a further 15 minutes. Remove the pan from the heat and carefully blend in the oysters and crabmeat.

- Spoon the mixture into individual ramekins, sprinkle with both cheeses, with a little smoked salmon. Top with breadcrumbs.

- Bake in the oven for 12 minutes.

- Serve with toasted garlic bread and finally top with a little caviare and a piece of lemon before serving.

- Without doubt worth the effort! Eat and enjoy what several chefs have been waiting for me to write.

INGREDIENTS

6 slices bread, trimmed & fried in garlic butter

3 dozen oysters in their natural juices

50g/2oz best butter

50g/2oz plain flour

300ml/10floz dry white wine

2 shallots finely chopped

15ml/1 tablespoon finely chopped parsley

15ml/1 teaspoon anchovy essence

salt

freshly milled black pepper

175g/6oz white crabmeat

75g/3oz creamy Lancashire cheese

75g/3oz Stilton cheese

125g/4oz smoked salmon

175g/6oz fresh breadcrumbs

1 small jar of caviare

1 lemon very thinly sliced

IRISH FISH CASSEROLE

*I*reland is one of the most picturesque places in Europe and I have friends from every corner of Great Britain who always enjoy visiting this part of the country not just for their favourite drink of Guinness but also for the cross border day trips to the Irish Riveria to taste the Kinsale oysters and onto Wicklow to see the salmon jumping.

— INGREDIENTS —

450g/1lb salmon fillet, skinned and chopped

450g/1lb hake fillet, skinned and chopped

75g/3oz Plain, seasoned flour

salt

freshly milled black pepper

75g/3oz best butter

4 shallots, skinned and finely chopped

1 carrot, peeled and diced

1 leek, washed, and finely chopped

300ml/½ pint dry white wine

300ml/½ pint of cider, medium sweet

10ml/2 teaspoons anchovy essence

15ml/1 tablespoon tarragon vinegar

chopped fresh parsley

— METHOD —

● Coat the fish in 25g/1oz of the seasoned flour. Melt the butter in a flameproof casserole and add the fish, onion, carrot and leeks cooking gently for 10 minutes.

● Sprinkle with the remaining flour, stirring for 2 minutes.

● Slowly add the cider, anchovy essence and tarragon vinegar. Bring to the boil and simmer for 35 minutes on a low heat or bake in the oven for 30 minutes at gas 4/350f/180c.

Sprinkle with freshly chopped parsley and serve with warm, crusty brown bread.

ENGLISH KEDGEREE

*K*nown as *Kitchri* and originally a spicy Indian recipe containing onions and lentils it was brought back to England for the breakfast table in the eighteenth century by the nabobs of the East India Company.

— METHOD —

● Flake the cooked finnan haddock, making sure all the bones and skin are removed.

● Melt the butter in medium saucepan and add the fish with a pinch of saffron. Chop the eggs and add them with the rice to the saucepan.

● Gently heat all the ingredients together, slowly add the cream, stirring thoroughly.

● Season with salt and freshly ground black pepper and serve hot with a sprinkle of freshly chopped parsley or coriander leaves.

— INGREDIENTS —

450g/1lb cooked finnan
Haddock, bone & skin removed

175g/6oz cooked
long-grain rice

salt

freshly ground black pepper

saffron powder

3 eggs, hard boiled and shelled

30ml/2 tablespoons
double cream

50g/2oz best butter

freshly chopped parsley

coriander leaves

*The Harbour,
Bridlington.*

CORNISH BUTTERED LOBSTER

A recipe dating from 1767 for buttered lobster. Cut the Lobster up small. Put it into a stewpan with a little gravy, butter, pepper, salt and vinegar. Set it over the fire till hot. Heat the shells, and serve the lobsters in them.

Mrs Rundell's 1846 cookery book adds a little nutmeg and flour to thicken. Patrick Lamb in his *Royal Cookery* book of 1710 uses the addition of minced anchovy and the lobster covered with paste.

— INGREDIENTS —

2 Large Lobsters about 700g each, split into halves

Juice and rind of 1 lemon

100g/4oz butter

4 tablespoons fresh white breadcrumbs

2 tablespoons brandy

5 tablespoons fresh double cream or creme fraise

salt

freshly milled black pepper

50g/2oz grated Cheddar cheese

2 lemons sliced

1 kiwi fruit sliced

4 king prawns, shell on cooked.

fresh sprigs dill

— METHOD —

● Carefully discard the stomach, veins and gills from each lobster.

● Remove all the meat from the tail and crack the claws and legs, removing the meat from them also.

● Place the meat chopped into a bowl and add the lemon juice and zest.

● Clean the shell thoroughly and place into a warm oven.

● Cook the breadcrumbs in 25g/1oz butter until crisp and golden brown, (about 3 minutes).

● Melt the remaining butter in a saucepan and gently heat the lobster meat, add the brandy and cook for a further 3 minutes. Add the cream, salt and freshly milled black pepper.

● Place the buttered lobster into the shells, cover with a little grated cheddar and the breadcrumbs grill for a few minutes until golden brown

Garnish with the slices of lemon and kiwi fruit, king prawns and sprigs of dill.

Mullion, 1924.

FERMANAGH TROUT WITH SMOKED BACON

I have a neighbour who goes fishing all the time and he brings me back some trout on nearly every trip; the flavour from wild trout is far superior to that of farmed. This makes an excellent barbecue recipe, which is how they would cooked it thousands of years ago in the British Isles. I love bacon and we have some of the finest curers on our doorstep without going abroad for it. British bacon is not injected with water and our Welsh and Northern Irish curers have some of the finest smoked bacon in Europe, always ask for Fermanagh smoked.

— INGREDIENTS —

4 x 275g/10oz wild trout, gutted and cleaned

salt

freshly milled black pepper

2 apples, peeled cored and sliced

4 sprigs of mint

juice of 1 lemon

12 rashers of smoked streaky bacon, rindless

25g/1oz butter

2 apples, cored and sliced

4 sprigs of freshly washed mint

— METHOD —

● PRE-HEAT the oven to gas 6/400f/200c.

● Open up the cavities of each trout and wash through thoroughly with warm salt water.

● Season each cavity with salt and freshly milled black pepper. Place equal amounts of sliced apple into the cavities with a sprig of mint.

● Squeeze the juice of the lemon over each cavity. Carefully cover the whole of the trout except the head and tail in a spiral with three rashers of smoked bacon.

● Grease a deep baking tray with the butter and place the trout on it, with the loose ends of bacon underneath. Season with freshly milled black pepper and bake for 20 minutes, turning the trout after 10 minutes.

● Remove them from the oven onto a serving dish and garnish with sliced apple and fresh mint.

Baked Scallops (Tanrogans)

Originally from the Isle of Man, the name Tanrogan was that of a scallop shell.

— Method —

- **Pre-heat** the oven to gas 4/350f/180c.

- Remove the scallops from their shells, scrape off the surrounding fringe (beard) and the black intestinal thread. The white part is the flesh and the orange part (coral) is the roe.

- Very carefully ease the flesh and coral from the shell with a short but very strong knife.

- Wash the shells thoroughly and dry them well.

- Place all twelve shells onto a baking sheet and place to one side for later.

- Put the scallops, fish stock, onion and freshly milled black pepper into a ovenproof baking dish, cover with cooking foil and bake for 8 minutes.

- Remove the foil and with a slotted spoon, replace the scallops into their shells. Add 1 tablespoon of the fish stock liquid to each shell with a squeeze of lemon, a little double cream and grated cheese to top each shell.

- Return the scallops to the oven for a further 4 minutes, turning up the oven to gas 8/450f/230c.

Serve the scallops on their own with crusty brown bread and butter.

— INGREDIENTS —

12 Scallops

150ml/¼ pint fish stock

1 onion, chopped

salt

freshly milled black pepper

juice and zest of 2 lemons

150ml/¼ double cream

200g/8oz grated Cheddar cheese

ROSA'S DEVILLED WHITEBAIT

*T*his recipe was always on the menu at The Cavendish Hotel, Jermyn Street, London. Rosa Lewis (the original Duchess of Duke Street) served it in a potato basket, garnished with prawns and fresh parsley, with triangles of fried bread dipped in chopped parsley with a sprinkling of Cayenne pepper, hence (Devilled) Whitebait. I do believe this recipe was taught to the great lady by Auguste Escoffier, who became a personal friend of Rosa's.

Whitebait today is readily available everywhere, but is mostly frozen and it is wise to spread them out on some kitchen paper to defrost being very careful not to break the tiny little things.

— INGREDIENTS —

450g/1lb fresh whitebait

300ml/½ pint fresh milk

100g/4oz plain white flour

1 teaspoon of salt

1 teaspoon cayenne pepper

freshly milled black pepper

cayenne

2 lemons sliced

sprigs fresh mint

— METHOD —

● Heat a deep frying pan half-filled with cooking oil to about 375f/190c (hot).

● Put the milk into a bowl and place the whitebait in the bowl for about 15 minutes. Meanwhile put the flour, salt, cayenne and a little freshly milled black pepper into a plastic bag and shake it well.

● Drain the whitebait being very careful not to break them.

● Place the flour mixture onto a large deep plate and gently toss the whitebait into the flour, again being very careful not to break the fish.

● Add about half the whitebait to the oil first, deep frying them for about 3 minutes until they a very crisp and golden brown.

● Place them onto some kitchen paper to drain and keep them warm. Repeat the process and then sprinkle with cayenne pepper. Garnish with lemon slices and sprigs of fresh mint.

Serve with slices of brown bread and butter and a glass of dry white wine.

NORTH STAFFORDSHIRE SWALLOWS

*T*his sandwich style fish recipe, comes from the Potteries, home of hot oat cakes and the finest crockery in Britain.

The idea is brilliant, it's like having fish and chips without the chips! A good beer batter with saffron and beef dripping is the only way this recipe should be made. If you're on a diet, make it for your family and friends with lots of salt and malt vinegar.

— METHOD —

• Slice the uncooked cod slightly smaller than the size of the sliced potato, to fit like a sandwich. Placing a slice of fish on a slice of potato, season well and cover with another slice of potato.

• Hold together with a cocktail stick.

• Heat the dripping in a large deep frying pan.

• Dip the cod sandwiches into the beer batter and fry for at least 5-6 minutes until golden brown, place them onto some paper kitchen towel to drain.

— INGREDIENTS —

450g/1lb cod fillet, skin removed

4 large potatoes, peeled and very thinly sliced, 3mm 1/8th inch

salt

freshly milled black pepper

cocktail sticks

BATTER INGREDIENTS
100g/4oz plain flour

pinch salt

2 eggs

275ml/1/2 pint milk

2 tablespoons of beer

1 tablespoon oil

pinch saffron

550g/1lb beef dripping

CLEDDAU SALMON & HADDOCK FISH CAKES

From the coastlines around Great Britain the fish cake packed its bags and moved from household to household for over 400 years. Then one day a chef by the name of Tom Bridge decided it was time we changed some of the recipe. But only the recipe, not the size! A fish cake should look like a fish cake and not be the size of a fifty pence piece.

— INGREDIENTS —

450g/1lb fresh salmon fillet, skin and any excess bones removed

450g/1lb fresh haddock fillet, skin and any excess bones removed

3 eggs, beaten

450g/1lb cooked potato, mashed

175g/6oz breadcrumbs

50ml/2 floz double cream

salt

freshly milled black pepper

beef dripping

— METHOD —

● Flake the raw fish and add it to the rest of the ingredients, blending them thoroughly in a mixer, a blender or by hand.

● Shape the mixture into fish cake shapes about 3cm/1 inch thick and about 7cm/3 inches wide.

● Place the fish cakes into hot dripping and fry them for 4 to 5 minutes until golden brown on both sides, drain them on kitchen paper and serve with a home-made tartar sauce.

Penmaenpool, 1913.

CASSEROLE OF SMOKED HADDOCK WITH EGG SAUCE

*T*his is a pre-Victorian recipe with all the gusto of everything that's British. Copied by food lovers around the world, the French call this *"Haddock Sauce aux Oeufs"*, they also use skate which is far too expensive to use in this sort of recipe, although you can use cod, monkfish or sole should you wish to do so.

— METHOD —

- PRE-HEAT the oven to gas 6/400f/200c.

- Use the first 25g/1oz butter to grease an ovenproof casserole dish and place the haddock fillets into it.

- Pour over the milk and cook for 15 minutes in the centre of the oven. Pour out the milk into a jug, being very careful not to break the fish in the casserole.

- Melt the other 25g/1oz butter in a saucepan and add the flour. Slowly whisk in the milk the fish was cooked in and season with the pepper and nutmeg.

- Stirring all the time, add the cream, parsley and finally the mashed egg. Cook for 2 minutes, blending thoroughly.

- Pour the sauce over the haddock and return to the oven for 8 minutes.

Serve with baby new potatoes and fresh boiled beetroot.

— INGREDIENTS —

450g/1lb smoked haddock, fillet, cut into 4 slices

25g/1oz butter

600ml/20floz milk

25g/1oz butter

25g/1oz plain flour

freshly milled black pepper

pinch freshly grated nutmeg

3 tablespoons double cream

1 tablespoon chopped parsley

2 eggs, boiled and mashed to a pulp

OLD FASHION FISH 'N' CHIPS

*H*ow could I possibly finish the fish section off without using my own recipe for fish and chips. Having been brought up on them it would be a shame not to use my mothers original recipe from when I lived in Hill Street in Bolton, Lancashire, at the tender age of 10 years.

The roots of this wonderful recipe come from Scarborough, Whitby and Bridlington where the haddock and cod are caught, that go into every fish and chip shop, in every town and every village across the Yorkshire and Lancashire borders.

— INGREDIENTS —

4 x 225g/8oz cod fillets

1 kg potatoes, peeled and chipped

dripping or sunflower cooking oil

salt

freshly ground white pepper

BATTER
200g/7oz plain flour

1 egg, whisked with 2 tablespoons beer

150ml/5floz milk and water mixed

salt

freshly milled white pepper

— METHOD —

● To make the batter, mix the flour, egg, milk and seasoning, whisking until it is very smooth and lump free. Leave it to stand for at least 1 hour.

● Heat the oil until it gives off a faint, almost invisible blue smoke (180c/350f). Fry the chips in small batches, when they start to brown remove them with a small slotted spoon or if you use a basket, the basket. Place them into a warm oven.

● Season each piece of fish, then dip into the batter, drawing it backwards and forwards 2 to 3 times to coat it fully.

● Then lower it gently into the hot fat, with skin side down to prevent the fish from curling.

● Fry the fish one at a time. After 5 minutes turn the fish over and cook, until brown for a further 3 minutes.

Traditionally they should be served on newspaper with salt and malt vinegar.

Chapter 4

MEAT

*I*f the British cook is to transform cookery, we must begin with herbs. It was a great French man, M. Andre Simon who said: *'A good cook is like a good actor; you cannot expect good cooking, any more than good acting, without a measure of applause....'*

Mint is one of those herbs that can transform food into a gourmet delight. Mint is in season from April to October. It has many uses, in soups, mint jelly, mint sauce, mint vinegar, mint yoghurt, mint julip, mint potatoes and my well-known apple and mint ice cream.

As a garnish it is without doubt, ideal for nearly every course, but one of the oldest recipes from the British cookery books is the use of mint stuffing. Here I have created a dish using breast of lakeland lamb.

John Chadwick's Family Butchers.

BREAST OF LAKELAND LAMB BAKED IN HONEY WITH MINT STUFFING

— INGREDIENTS —

900g/2lb lamb breast

5ml/1 teaspoon ground ginger

30ml/2 tablespoons clear honey

30g/1 best butter

1 onion, finely chopped

1 egg, beaten

30ml/2 tablespoons port

100g/4oz fresh breadcrumbs

60ml/4 tablespoons finely chopped fresh mint

30ml/2 tablespoons chopped parsley

salt

freshly ground black peppercorns

— METHOD —

● Melt the butter in a frying pan and fry the onion until soft.

● In a separate bowl, beat the egg with the port and blend in the breadcrumbs, ginger, parsley and mint. Add the onions and season the mixture with salt and freshly ground black pepper.

● Flatten the meat and remove all the excess fat. Place the mixture onto the meat, then roll up the meat tightly and secure it with some butchers string.

● Place the lamb onto a large piece of cooking foil, warm the honey and pour over the lamb, securing the foil around the lamb so the honey and lamb juices do not escape.

● Cook in a hot oven, gas 8/230c/450f for 35-40 minutes.

● Very carefully remove the foil, retaining the juices, placing them into a saucepan.

● Return the meat to the oven for a further 15 minutes to brown.

● Put some more finely chopped mint into the saucepan with the juice and add 15ml/1tablespoon of port. Bring to the boil and allow to simmer for 10 minutes.

● Strain the sauce through a fine sieve into a sauce boat and serve with the breast of lamb.

STILTON STEAKS

Stilton Cheese and vintage port is a natural marriage, and in sickness and in health, I have always been blessed with having this course to end most of my evening meals. Stilton, the 'King' of English cheese is covered by a Certification Trade Mark which ensures that it is only made in the three shires of Leicester, Derby and Nottingham.
In the eighteenth century it is reputed to have been made at Quenby Hall in Leicestershire and to have been known there as Lady Beaumont's cheese. The reputed cheese passed through many hands before finally arriving in Stilton, where it was sold at the Bell Inn by Cooper Thornhill.

Both the cheese and the name go back even further than that. In Pope's, *Imitations of Horace,* these lines appear in the course of a reference to Prior's story of the town mouse and the country mouse:
Cheese, such as men in Suffolk make,
But wish'd it Stilton for his sake.

This takes Stilton back to George II. A Stilton should be cut before it is over-ripe and should be finished before it goes dry. It should be sliced horizontally to expose the least extent of the surface to drying. This way the last piece of the cheese will be quite moist. If your cheese is drying, then I suggest adding a little port to the cheese and wrapping it in a damp cloth/serviette.

What is the right port to drink with Stilton? I like an Old Tawny other recommendations are Madeira, Sweet Sherry or a Sauterne. After this very brief introduction to Stilton, do try my Stilton & Green Peppercorn Steaks on the following page.

Derby Cathedral from St Mary's Gate, 1896.

STILTON & GREEN PEPPERCORN STEAKS

— INGREDIENTS —

1 tablespoon sesame oil

4 x 225g/8oz 2.5cm/1inch thick sirloin steaks

freshly milled black pepper

salt

2 tablespoons brandy

1 tablespoon green peppercorns

175g/6oz crumbled Stilton cheese

3 tablespoons double cream

1 tablespoon parsley, finely chopped

— METHOD —

● PRE-HEAT the oven to gas 6/400f/200c.

● Heat the oil in the frying pan, trim and season each steak and fry the steaks for 3 minutes on either side. Add the brandy and set it alight.

● When the flames have disappeared, remove the steaks to a ovenproof serving dish and keep warm in the oven.

● Add the rest of the ingredients to the juices in the frying pan. Bring to the boil blending everything together and then pour the sauce over the steaks.

Clock Tower & Eastgates, Leicester.

BEEF WELLINGTON

*O*r is it Bronte's Pie? Writing to her sister, Emily, on December 1st, 1843, Charlotte recalled how she would like to be in the kitchen at Haworth Parsonage, cutting up the hash and topping this with pastry; it would then be baked in the oven.

— METHOD —

● With a sharp knife, trim the fat from the beef fillet or sirloin.

● Season the meat well with salt and ground black pepper.

● Melt the butter in a large frying pan and add the beef, sealing the meat all over, cooking for at least 8 minutes. Remove the fillet from the pan, and place it to one side.

● In the same pan add a little more butter and the chopped onion and mushrooms, cooking until all the moisture has evaporated. Allow them to cool.

● Pre-set the oven to gas 6/200c/400f.

● Roll out the pastry to a large rectangle and place onto a greased baking sheet.

● Spread the onion and mushroom mixture onto the centre of the pastry and place the beef onto the mixture.

● Top the fillet with a layer of pâté.

● Brush the edges of the pastry with the beaten egg and fold and seal the pastry, pressing the edges together well.

● Make some flowers and leaves from the leftover pastry to decorate the wellington and brush it completely with the beaten egg.

● Bake in the centre of the oven for 20 minutes, then lower the oven to gas 4/350f/180c for a further 15 minutes, until golden brown.

— INGREDIENTS —

Serves 6-8

900g/2lb fillet or sirloin of beef

75g/3oz butter

1 onion, finely chopped

175g/6oz button or wild mushrooms

450g/1lb puff pastry

175g/6oz chicken liver pâté

1 egg, lightly beaten

salt

freshly ground black pepper

— CHEF'S — ALTERNATIVE TIP

Should you not be a lover of red meat, try this same recipe with breast of turkey, chicken or pork fillet using a lambs liver pâté for the turkey or chicken.

ROAST LOIN OF IRISH PORK

*T*he Irish really have the edge with their Limerick hams and pork. With evergreen pastures, the sheep of Wicklow also enjoy the lush country that brings us the flavours of this wonderful island.

I love pork crackling and to make perfect pork crackling you must score it evenly. It is simple, all you do is to penetrate the skin and a little of the fat below it with a very sharp knife, making diamond shape cuts about 1cm-½ inch square. Gently brush the pork with a little oil and salt the crackling all over generously. It is then ready for roasting.

— INGREDIENTS —

Serves 4-6

2lb - 6lb loin of Irish pork

fresh rosemary

bay leaves

coarse salt

freshly ground black pepper

honey

— METHOD —

It is important that you adhere to the cooking time of 30 minutes per 450g/1lb. Traditional roast loin of pork, cooked with rosemary, served with apple sauce, sage & onion stuffing, crackling and pork gravy. For the Lowry Irish Clan.

- PRE-HEAT the oven to gas 8/230c/450f.

- To get the crackling really crisp, place the joint, skin side down, in a roasting tray and pour in about 1 inch of boiling water.

- Place the tray into the centre of the oven and cook for 20 minutes. Remove the tray, pour off the liquid and use it for basting the pork.

- Place the pork back into the roasting tin, skin side up. Season and add a few bay leaves and some rosemary into the score marks.

- Reduce the heat to gas 4/180c/350f.

- Cook for 30 minutes to the pound, basting every 20 minutes. Allow it to cool then remove the crackling. Cut it into long thin strips and place onto a baking tray. Salt and coat with a little honey and cook for a further 10 minutes.

Garnish the plate with apple sauce and sage and onion stuffing.
Place the slices of pork and crackling into a fanned circle and serve hot or cold.

CROWN OF WICKLOW LAMB WITH WHITE PUDDING GARNISH

With lamb in abundance, it is without doubt one of the most popular cuts of meat in the Irish and British cookery calendar. Once a month I treat myself in restaurants, trying different versions and recipes using this wonderful meat. I still feel this is the classical Irish recipe and far superior to the modern version.

— METHOD —

- PRE-HEAT the oven to gas 4/180c/350f.

- Trim each cutlet bone to a depth of 2.5cm/1 inch with a sharp knife.

- Bend the joints around, fat side inwards to form a crown.

- Cover each exposed bone with cooking foil and place into a small baking tray.

- Slowly melt the butter in a saucepan, add the onion, rosemary, apple and pear and cook for 4 minutes. Add the breadcrumbs, mint and egg and season well.

- Fill the centre of the crown with the stuffing. Cover the crown with cooking foil and bake for 80 minutes.

- Ten minutes before the end of cooking time, remove the foil and pour the honey around the sides of the crown, not touching the top. Replace the foil and continue the cooking process.

- Grill the white pudding for 3 minutes either side.

Garnish with slices of grilled white pudding, fresh shallots glazed with the honey, juices from the lamb and baked parsnip with mint and onion gravy.

— INGREDIENTS —

2 best end necks of lamb, with 6 cutlets, chinned on each

1 tablespoon butter

1 onion, finely chopped

1 teaspoon freshly ground rosemary

1 eating apple, cored and chopped

1 pear, cored and chopped

100g/4oz fresh breadcrumbs

2 tablespoons freshly chopped mint

1 egg

salt
freshly milled black pepper

3 tablespoons clear honey

4 x 100g/4oz slices of white pudding, grilled

LANCASHIRE SIRLOIN OF ENGLISH BEEF ROASTED WITH A HERB CRUST & A MUSTARD SEED YORKSHIRE PUDDING

When Sir Richard Hoghton invited King James I to have a little lunch at Hoghton Tower near Preston, we would never have known that a new word was to be added to the culinary dictionary. Brought to the table on that day of festivities was a magnificent loin of beef which took the King's fancy, so much so he knighted it there and then saying "Arise Sir Loin of Beef".

— INGREDIENTS —

50g/2oz beef dripping, melted

1.4kg/3lb sirloin of beef

75g/3oz breadcrumbs

2 teaspoons mixed herbs

a pinch Madras curry powder

Yorkshire Pudding Batter
(see recipe page 37)
into which you whisk in 2
tablespoons of mustard seed

— METHOD —

●   PRE-HEAT the oven to gas 4/180c/350f.

●   Trim the excess fat from the beef and place into a shallow baking tin on the melted dripping,

●   Mix the rest of the ingredients in a bowl to make a paste. Cover the top of the sirloin, then roast in the oven for 70 minutes.

●   Increase the oven temperature to gas 7/220c/425f. Put the rest of the dripping into a large baking tray and place into the oven for 3 minutes until the dripping is smoking.

●   Pour in the Yorkshire/mustard seed batter and bake for 30 minutes.

●   Remove both the meat and Yorkshire pudding. Carve the beef, make a gravy with the beef juices and serve with the mustard seed Yorkshire pudding.

Hoghton Towers, 1895.

CORNED BEEF HASH

*T*his is one of those recipes you see in every cafe throughout Great Britain. I remember a winter's day in Lowestoft, a little cafe near the station. I ordered a cup of tea and all I could smell was fried onion. I asked the waitress what they were cooking and she said a corned beef hash for lunch; I returned an hour later to enjoy a taste of tradition.

— INGREDIENTS —

450g/1lb tin corned beef

25g/1oz beef dripping

1 large onion, chopped roughly

600ml/1 pint beef stock,
thicken with a little cornstarch

1 tablespoon mushroom
ketchup

900g/2lb cooked and mashed
potatoes (buttered & seasoned)

50g/2oz butter, melted

75g/3oz grated Cheddar cheese

freshly ground black pepper

— METHOD —

● PRE-HEAT the oven to gas 4/180c/350f.

● Chop the cooked corned beef into half inch cubes and place into a casserole dish. Gently fry the onions in a little dripping then add to top the dish. Sprinkle with mushroom ketchup, and cover with beef stock.

● Top with the mashed potato, melted butter and grated cheese. Season with freshly milled black pepper.

● Bake until golden brown for 20 to 25 minutes.

Sudbury Market, 1904.

WILTSHIRE PORK CUTLETS

*W*iltshire is still very popular for pork. One the most famous recipes during the eighteenth century from this area is *Love in Disguise*, which was calves' heart filled with a pork forcemeat, coated in breadcrumbs and baked in the oven. This is quite a simple nineteenth century recipe, that could possibly have been served during a hunt supper. This area was known as the Kingdom of the Pig and every choice cut is used in the making of pies, sausages, and hams. The alternative for this dish is to use veal cutlets, should you not like using pork.

— METHOD —

- PRE-HEAT the oven to gas 2/300f/150c.

- Melt the butter in a large frying pan and gently fry the cutlets for 5 minutes either side. Remove the cutlets from the pan and place onto a dish. Keep them warm in the oven.

- In the same frying pan, fry the onions and apple slices together, browning the apple slightly.

- Place the apple and onions onto a serving dish, arrange the cutlets, placing them onto the onion and apple slices. Keep warm in the oven.

- In the same frying pan, melt the remaining butter and gently fry the mushrooms, coriander and peppercorns. Cook for 3 minutes then sprinkle the sesame seeds onto the mushrooms.

- Place the mushroom, peppercorns and juices onto the cutlets and arrange the tomatoes around the edge of the cutlets. Return to the oven for a further 5 minutes.

- Season well with salt and freshly milled black pepper and garnished with coriander leaves before serving.

— INGREDIENTS —

50g/2oz butter

4 x 250g/9oz pork cutlets, trimmed

1 large onion, sliced

2 apples, peeled, cored and sliced

25g/1oz butter

175g/6oz button mushrooms

1 tablespoon chopped coriander leaves

8 black peppercorns

1 tablespoon sesame seeds

2 large tomatoes, cut in half

salt

freshly milled black pepper

coriander leaves

NORFOLK FARMHOUSE GRILL

*N*orfolk really is the battling ground for farm country and nowhere else in Great Britain will you find the wives of the farmers, tucking into this superb grill but in Norfolk. It is also a fishing area, and one of the places I loved to visit was Lowestoft for smoked herrings and fresh crabs. So if you wish to have a seafood grill, try tasting some of the finest fish from the Norfolk coast line.

— INGREDIENTS —

Serves 4

4 lamb cutlets, trimmed

4 pork sausages

4 x 175g/6oz rump steak

4 x 100g/4oz gammon steak

1 ring black pudding
cut into four, skin removed

2 lambs or pigs kidneys,
cut into halves

225g/8oz button mushrooms

2 large beef tomatoes

salt

freshly milled black pepper

fresh watercress for garnish

4 x rings of pineapple
or 4 poached eggs

— METHOD —

● Season all the meats well with salt and freshly milled pepper.

● Grill all the meats until cooked for approx 4 minutes either side. Grill or fry the black pudding for 3 minutes either side.

● Place them onto a large serving dish and keep them hot in a warm oven.

● Into a large frying pan add 2 tablespoons of cooking oil and gently fry the mushrooms and tomatoes for 3 minutes.

● Place them around the meats and garnish with some watercress. Top the gammon steaks with a fresh ring of pineapple or a poached egg.

A Very 'W.I.S.E' Recipe

*A*nother one of my slightly expensive creations, but it does serve about 6-8 people and is a really nice party piece. The meat must be sliced to look like small, flat cakes. Instead of veal, you could consider using Norfolk turkey fillet or Lincolnshire duck breast.

— Method —

- **Pre-heat** the oven to gas 2/300f/150c.

- Melt the butter and oil in a large frying pan and fry each cut of meat off for 4 minutes either side. Season well with salt and freshly milled black pepper and place onto a large tray (remembering what each cut of meat is). Place into the oven to keep warm.

- Using the same pan, cook the leeks for 3 minutes and place to one side.

- Arrange the leeks, potato, haggis and black pudding around the edge of a large serving dish. Placing the slices of lamb onto the leeks, pork onto potato, beef onto haggis and veal onto the black pudding. Leaving the centre of the plate empty, spread the cabbage onto the base of the centre and return to the oven for 12 minutes.

- Meanwhile fry the mushrooms for 4 minutes in the same pan juices and fat, sprinkle with flour and cook for 2 further minutes. Add the beef stock, cream and whisky, stirring continuously. Season with salt and freshly milled black pepper.

Place the mushrooms and the sauce into the centre of the serving dish onto the shredded cabbage, garnish with fresh watercress and serve with NOTHING ELSE!

— INGREDIENTS —

225g/8oz of the following meats: trimmed and cut into 50g/2oz pieces (rosettes)
Welsh lamb fillet
Irish pork fillet
Scotch beef fillet
English veal fillet

50g/2oz butter

50g/2oz sunflower oil

225g/8oz leeks sliced

225g/8oz potato, cooked and sliced

100g/4oz haggis, cooked and sliced

100g/4oz black pudding, sliced

225g/8oz Savoy cabbage, very finely shredded, cooked

225g/8oz button mushrooms

25g/1oz plain flour

150ml/5floz beef stock

4 tablespoons double cream

2 tablespoons Drambuie whisky

salt

freshly milled black pepper

1 large bunch of watercress

VICTORIAN POT ROAST BEEF

*"In days of old when Knights were bold and cookers hadn't been invented
    They dug a hole in the middle of the ground and cooked their hearts contented"*

This very ancient dish is one of those that was copied by every cook and chef. Queen Victoria's chef, Charles Elme Francatelli, claimed this to be his own recipe! It was then called *"Braised Beef a la Polonaise aux Choux Rouges"*. My version is a little more modernised, but the flavours and method are still Victorian and it is a regular feature on my dinner table.

— INGREDIENTS —

1.4 kg/3 lb topside of beef

50g/2oz butter

20 shallots, peeled.

4 large potatoes,
peeled and quartered

2 large carrots, peeled and
cut into chunks

2 parsnips, peeled and
cut into chunks

1 small turnip, peeled and chopped

1 sprig fresh thyme

1 sprig rosemary

salt

freshly milled black pepper

300ml/10floz beef stock

150ml/5floz good quality red wine
(not plonk)

2 tablespoons cornflour blended with
a little red wine

— METHOD —

● Quickly fry the topside of beef off in the butter, browning well all over, then place to one side.

● Fry the shallots, potatoes, carrot, parsnip and turnip in the butter and beef juice. Then place the beef, surrounded by the vegetables into a large, deep casserole/pot. Add all the rest of the ingredients, except the cornflour.

● Cover with a lid or cooking foil, place into the centre of the oven and cook for 2 hours. Half an hour before the meat is cooked, remove the lid or foil to allow the meat to brown a little more.

● Carefully place the meat and vegetables onto a large serving dish, remove the thyme and rosemary sprigs and bring the stock juices to the boil. Add the cornflour, blended with a little wine.

● Cook and simmer for 4 minutes pour around the vegetables and serve, garnished with fresh thyme.

Rabbit Stew with Guinness & Norfolk Dumplings

*A*nother national institution, having beef stew without dumplings, is like having roast beef without Yorkshire pudding, *I could just not face life!* Every town and village throughout Great Britain has their own versions. This is one of those really old village recipes from yester-year.

— Method —

● Toss the rabbit in the seasoned flour, heat the dripping in a large saucepan and fry the rabbit and onions for 5 minutes. Add the beef stock and stout, seasoning well with salt and freshly milled black pepper.

● Bring the contents to the boil and remove any excess scum floating on the surface. Add the rest of the ingredients except the dumplings. Stew slowly for 2 hours.

● Add the dumplings and cook for a further 30 minutes.

Serve this with a glass of cider.

— INGREDIENTS —

900g/2lb rabbit, diced, fat and gristle removed

50g/2oz flour, well seasoned

50g/2oz beef dripping

2 onions, peeled and sliced

600ml/20floz beef stock

salt

freshly milled black pepper

150ml/5floz Guinness

2 large potatoes, peeled and diced

1 large carrot, peeled and diced

175g/6oz button mushrooms, sliced

175g/6oz peas

dumplings *(recipe on page 19)*

PAN FRIED WELSH LAMB LIVER, ONIONS & BACON

*T*his recipe is for everyone at Waterton Press, especially Louise, who worked with me so hard on the design and presentation of this wonderful cookbook.

— INGREDIENTS —

Serves 4

450lb/16oz Welsh lambs liver, thinly sliced

salt

freshly milled black pepper

25g/1oz plain flour

25g/1oz cooking oil

25g/1oz dripping

2 onions, sliced

225g/8oz smoked streaky bacon, rindless

150ml/5floz good rich gravy

— METHOD —

● Season the liver with salt and freshly milled black pepper and dust with the flour.

● Heat the oil and dripping and fry the liver quickly on both sides so that the liver remains pink. Remove the liver from the pan and keep it warm.

● Add the onions and bacon to the pan and cook for 4 minutes. Add the gravy and simmer for 5 minutes. Return the liver and the juices to the pan and simmer for a further 5 minutes.

● Arrange slices of the liver, onion and bacon onto individual warm plates, strain the sauce through a non-metallic sieve and pour around the liver.

Serve with new potatoes and button mushrooms.

Town Hall, Bridgend, 1899.

LAMB CUTLETS REFORM

*J*nvented in the 1830's for the London Reform Club by famous French chef, Alexis Sayer, who worked with Florence Nightingale during the Crimean War, setting up the Soup Kitchens for the hospitals and Armed Forces. His version of this famous sauce was, I feel too strong for the British palette, so I have modified the recipe slightly.

— METHOD —

- For the sauce, melt the butter in a saucepan, add the onion, carrot and ham and cook gently for 5 minutes. Pour in the vinegar and port, bring the sauce to the boil and reduce by half.

- Lower the heat on the pan and add the stock, mace, cloves, rosemary, bay leaf and juniper berries. Bring to the boil and then gently simmer the sauce for 35 minutes.

- Mix the minced ham and breadcrumbs together, coat each cutlet with the beaten egg and then coat them in the ham and breadcrumb mixture.

- Pan fry the cutlets in the butter, for about 5 minutes either side, until golden brown and place onto a warm serving dish. Keep warm in a low oven until the sauce is ready.

- After the sauce has simmered for 35 minutes, remove the bay leaf and sprig of rosemary add the cornflour, and blended with a little port, to the saucepan, stirring constantly until the sauce thickens. Let it simmer for a further 5 minutes.

- Remove the cutlets from the oven and place a cutlet frill or a piece of tin foil around each cutlet, pour the sauce into a sauceboat and serve with broccoli and new potatoes.

— INGREDIENTS —

25g/1oz butter

1 large onion, finely chopped

1 carrot, sliced (matchstick)

50g/2oz York ham, cut into very thin strips

3 tablespoons red wine vinegar

3 tablespoons port

600ml/20 floz chicken stock

pinch mace

2 cloves

1 sprig rosemary

1 bay leaf

5 juniper berries, crushed

8 x 100g/4oz lamb cutlets, bone completely trimmed and clean to within 2.5cm/1 inch of the meat.

75g/3oz York ham, finely minced

75g/3oz fresh breadcrumbs

1 egg, beaten with 1 tablespoon of milk

50g/2oz butter

1 tablespoon cornflour blended with a little port

LOBSCOUSE

I have relatives all over Liverpool and they have to be the friendliest, most humourous and warm people I have ever met. The Melia family eat Scouse while singing the Crystal Chandelier.

I have made this recipe for the Beatles, Gerry & The Pacemakers, Cilla Black, Jimmy Tarbuck and Ken Dodd, to name a few of the Liverpudlians who really do enjoy a pan of scouse. This recipe was given to me by my father-in-law, Jim Fitzpatrick, who lived in Bootle. The dockers at Liverpool came home to this after a solid weeks work, then it was off to the pub for a well deserved pint.

Again the recipes vary all over the country for Lobscouse, some just use silverside, some add peas and some add swede. This is about the best and tastiest recipe I have ever come across and my wife Jayne, who is a Liverpool Belle, swears this is the original recipe!

For *Doreen Fitzpatrick,* Park Lane, Bootle.

— INGREDIENTS —

900g/2lb neck of lamb, fat removed and cut into cubes, then soaked in 600ml/1 pint beef stock overnight

450g/1lb stewing steak, fat removed and cubed

50g/2oz dripping

3 large onions, peeled and sliced

900g/2lb potatoes, peeled and sliced

2 carrots, peeled and sliced

salt

freshly milled black pepper

— METHOD —

● PRE-HEAT the oven gas 3/325f/170c.

● Melt the beef dripping in a deep ovenproof casserole.

● Remove the lamb from the beef stock and dry the meat in some paper kitchen towel.

● Seal the lamb and beef quickly in the hot dripping, add the onions and cook for 6 minutes.

● *LOB* all the ingredients into the casserole, adding the beef stock and just enough water to just cover the ingredients.

● Place a lid onto the casserole or cover with cooking foil and cook in the centre of the oven for 4 hours,until the scouse is completely cooked and blended together.

● For *BLIND SCOUSE* add an extra assortment of vegetables 900g/2lb, omitting the meat.

WORDSWORTH BACON & APPLE HOTPOT

*E*very county has their own hot pot, especially Lancashire which follows this recipe. Northern Ireland have a *Coddle* which uses sausages and lamb and Cumbrians use bacon and apple, which is surprisingly very good. I visit Grasmere quite often each year and one of the finest hotels in that area is the Nanny Brow Country House Hotel at Clappersgate near Ambleside. Well worth a visit.

— METHOD —

● Soak the cubed bacon in cold water for 5 hours, remove from the water and dry.

● Place all the ingredients except the 8 dumplings into a large saucepan, bring to the boil and simmer on a low heat for 1 hour, 30 minutes.

● Remove any excess scum from the pan. Add the dumplings and simmer for a further 25 minutes, then serve with cabbage and crusty brown bread.

Old Windmill, Parbold.

— INGREDIENTS —

1.4 kg/3lb boiling bacon, fat removed, trimmed and cubed

450g/1lb Granny Smith apples, peeled, cored and thinly sliced

2 large onions, peeled and sliced

2 large carrots, peeled and sliced

1 small turnip, peeled and sliced

2 tablespoons of black treacle

4 large potatoes, peeled and sliced

pinch mace, sage & thyme

freshly milled black pepper and salt to taste

1 ltr of chicken stock

8 dumplings, *(see oxtail soup recipe on page 19)*

TRADITIONAL LANCASHIRE HOTPOT

A quote from Florence White's *Good Things In England, 1932.*
"Manchester is noted for its hot-pots and has a special one of its own but the following excellent recipe hails from Bolton-le-Moors. (Bowton). The oysters may be omitted, but they are the correct thing in a real hot-pot.
Another correct thing is to serve Lancashire hot-pot with a dish or glass jar of pickled red cabbage whatever recipe be used. This is traditional".

— INGREDIENTS —

BOLTON HOTPOT AUTHOR'S
REVISED RECIPE
50g/2oz dripping

900g/2lb middle neck of mutton, trimmed and cut into chops

2 large onions, peeled and sliced

25g/1oz plain flour

600ml/20floz beef stock

salt

freshly milled black pepper

100g/4oz lambs kidney, diced

225g/8oz button mushrooms

10 oysters, washed and beard removed (optional)

900g/2lb potatoes, peeled and thinly sliced

— METHOD —

- PRE-HEAT the oven gas 5/375f/190c.

- Heat the dripping in a large frying pan and quickly brown the chops, cooking for about 3 minutes.

- Move the chops to a large ovenproof casserole with a lid and keep them warm in a low oven.

Fry the onions until they become transparent, about 3 minutes. Add the flour and cook for 2 minutes, then slowly add the beef stock and season well with salt and pepper, stirring all the time.

- Remove the chops from the oven and place the kidneys, mushrooms and oysters with the chops, layering them with the potatoes.

- Pour over the onion stock and cook in the centre of the oven for 2 hours.

- Take off the lid during the last 15 minutes to brown the potatoes.

IRISH CODDLE

*F*or well over 100 years *McCartney's Family Butchers* have been supplying award winning sausages to their customers from around the world, myself being one of them. With over 35 varieties you will find it very hard to make a choice which should be used for a coddle. The Main street of Moira in County Down would be queuing on Friday morning for their world famous Traditional Beef which has won the best sausage award in Northern Ireland four times.

— METHOD —

● Heat the lard or dripping in a large saucepan and gently fry the sausage, bacon, kidney and onions for 6 minutes. Add the flour and cook for 1 minute, slowly add the chicken stock and Guinness stirring constantly.

● Add the potatoes and season well with salt and freshly milled black pepper. Simmer on a low heat stirring every 15 minutes for 90 minutes.

Serve with Irish soda bread and a pint of Guinness.

Irish Street, Downpatrick, 1900.

— INGREDIENTS —

50g/2oz lard or dripping

450g/1lb Irish sausage

175g/6oz Irish back bacon, rindless and chopped

175g/6oz lambs kidney, chopped

2 large onions, peeled and sliced

25g/1oz plain flour

600ml/1 pint chicken stock

150ml/5floz Guinness

900g/2lb potatoes, peeled and chopped

salt

freshly milled black pepper

SHREWSBURY LAMB CUTLETS

— INGREDIENTS —

8 x100g/4oz loin of lamb cutlets, trimmed

25g/1oz butter

100g/4oz button mushrooms, sliced

100g/4oz shallots, peeled and sliced

4 tablespoons redcurrant jelly

1 tablespoon Worcestershire sauce

juice of 1 lemon

25g/1oz plain flour

300ml/10floz beef stock

1 sprig mint, finely chopped

pinch nutmeg

salt

freshly milled black pepper

1 sprig mint

1 bunch redberries

— METHOD —

● PRE-HEAT the oven gas 3/325f/170c.

● Melt the butter in a frying pan and brown the cutlets on both sides, cooking for about 4 minutes.

● Place the cutlets into a large casserole with the mushrooms and shallots. Add the redcurrant jelly, Worcestershire sauce and lemon juice to the frying pan. Add the flour and blend thoroughly to make a smooth paste. Cook for 3 minutes.

● Slowly add the beef stock and cook for 10 minutes. Add the mint and nutmeg and season well with salt and freshly milled black pepper.

● Pour the sauce over the cutlets and cook in the centre of the oven for 90 minutes.

Serve this with fresh oatcakes and garnish the casserole with a sprig of fresh mint and the red berries.

High Street, Shrewsbury, 1931.

SAUSAGE & MASH WITH ONION GRAVY

*A*nother one of those recipes that you would see in every type of restaurant. I even tried this in a French Brasserie in Manchester run by a dear friend of mine, Francis Carroll, who was born in Belgium. Now there's a combination for you! Although his wonderful mother does live in Paris and I think that's were he gets his talent from!

Use your favourite sausages for this recipe, mine being Lincolnshire, Irish and Cumberland; the fame of our British banger will never die.

METHOD

- PRE-HEAT the oven to gas 2/300f/150c.

- Heat the oil or dripping in a large frying pan. Prick the sausages with a fork in three different places and gently fry them, cooking them until golden brown all over for about 6 minutes.

- Place the sausages into a deep serving dish and put them into the oven to keep warm.

- Meanwhile, re-heat the boiled potatoes. Melt the butter in a large saucepan and gently fry the onion for 3 minutes.

- Strain the boiled potatoes and mash them with the onions and butter. Add the parsley a little freshly grated nutmeg and salt to taste. Blend the potatoes and place into another serving dish and keep warm in the oven.

Recipe for the Onion gravy on next page.

INGREDIENTS

25g/1oz cooking oil or dripping

12 thick Lincolnshire sausages

900g/2lb potatoes, peeled and boiled

50g/2oz butter

1 onion, peeled and chopped

1 tablespoon chopped parsley

freshly grated nutmeg

salt

AUTHOR'S RECIPE - ONION GRAVY

For Francis Carroll

*T*his is a recipe that I have been using for years and it is taken from my *200 Classic Sauces* published by Cassell.

— INGREDIENTS —

2 large onions, peeled & sliced

50g/2oz dripping

50g/2oz plain flour

2 rashers of best back bacon
(rind & gristle removed)

600ml/1 pint of beef stock

bouquet garni

1 tablespoon tomato paste

2 tablespoons of British sherry

salt

60ml/$^1/_2$ tablespoon red wine
vinegar

freshly ground black pepper

pinch of salt

— METHOD —

●   Chop the bacon rashers finely. Melt the dripping in a heavy based pan and add the bacon and onions, cooking for 6 minutes until light brown. Add the sherry and vinegar and cook for 3 minutes.

●   Blend in the flour, stirring the roux until it is brown. Gradually add half the beef stock, stirring constantly until the mixture has cooked through and thickened. Add the bouquet garni and simmer for 30 minutes. Add the tomato paste, seasoning and beef stock, simmering and skimming for a further 30 minutes.

●   Check and re-check the seasoning all the time.

●   Strain through a fine sieve, skim off any extra fat, pour over the sausages and serve with the mash.

When I am serving onion gravy for Yorkshire pudding's, I always add the juice from the roast beef to the above with an extra finely chopped onion.

Mill & River, Norfolk Broads, c.1934.

BEEF OLIVES

*T*his is one of those recipes from the Middle Ages that was transformed through time. It started life being a filling for a full side of beef, veal, lamb and wild boar. Then it was transformed into escalopes of meat, fish and game through the centuries, because it was far easier to cook.
You will need some butchers string, strong thread or wooden cocktail sticks.

— INGREDIENTS —

STUFFING

175g/6oz fine breadcrumbs

1 tablespoon anchovy essence

4 tablespoons finely chopped onion

2 tablespoons ham, finely chopped

1 teaspoon parsley

1 teaspoon thyme

salt

freshly milled black pepper

1 beaten with 1 tablespoon brandy

OLIVES & SAUCE

8 x 175g/6 oz sirloin beef escalopes

600ml/20floz beef stock

12 shallots, peeled

25g/1oz butter

25g/1oz flour

2 tablespoons port

2 tablespoon red wine

salt

freshly milled black pepper

— METHOD —

● PRE-HEAT the oven to gas 4/350f/180c.

● Place all the ingredients for the stuffing into a large mixing bowl and blend thoroughly for about 3 minutes. Roll the mixture into 8 large balls and place to one side.

● Flatten the steaks with a steak tenderiser or heavy rolling pin until they are very thin.

● Place the stuffing onto the centre of the meat and spread it all over, then roll the meat up into a Swiss roll shape. Tie each olive like a parcel or skewer with wooden cocktail sticks holding the meat to keep its shape.

● Lay the olives into a lightly greased ovenproof casserole, put in the beef stock and shallots, cover the dish and bake in the centre of the oven for 30 minutes.

● Carefully lift the beef olives from the casserole onto a warm serving dish, remove the string or cocktail sticks, surround with the shallots and keep warm.

● Melt the butter into a saucepan, add the flour and cook for 3 minutes. Add the beef stock from the olives and bring to the boil. Let the sauce simmer then add the port and red wine. Season with salt and pepper and allow to simmer for 5 minutes.

● Pour the port and wine sauce over the beef olives and serve with new potatoes and crusty brown bread.

Chapter 5

POULTRY & GAME

*G*reat Britain is a haven for all types of poultry and game. I personally have tried and tasted every game bird in the British Isles. Most of these are my favourite dishes that I have devised or developed for major food companies throughout the UK.

I would like to thank Les and everyone at Makentie in Newburgh, Lancashire for their Fowl advice, their chixs are Booooooooootiful!

Delivering Milk, Staithes, c.1925.

SUPREME OF CHICKEN NELL GWYN

A very saucy recipe, named after the mistress of Charles II, who was an orange seller outside the Covent Garden Theatre. I first served this in 1976 to Dr Donald Coggan, the then Archbishop of Canterbury, who found it very amusing. I last served it to HRH Prince Charles during the Prince's Trust Dinner, who said, "It was an excellent conversation piece".

— INGREDIENTS —

25g/1oz butter

15 ml/1 tablespoon olive oil

15g/½ oz plain flour

4 x 225g/8oz chicken supremes

30 ml/2 tablespoons chopped fresh tarragon

150ml/5floz fresh orange juice

3 fresh oranges, cut into segments and rind cut into very fine strips (julienne)

25g/2oz courgettes, cut into very fine strips

25g/2ozs red peppers, cut into very fine strips

25g/2oz shredded leeks

150ml/5floz orange brandy

salt and freshly milled black pepper

150ml/5floz fromage frais

— METHOD —

● Heat the butter and oil in a large frying pan, add the supremes and cook quickly until light golden brown all over.

● Add the orange brandy and cook for 2 minutes. Sprinkle lightly with the flour and cook for a further minute.

● Reduce the heat and add the orange juice, courgettes, peppers and leeks. Season with salt and freshly milled black pepper and simmer for 4 minutes, until the orange sauce is reduced and thickens.

● Add half the segments, rind, tarragon and fromage frais. Cook for a further 2 minutes.

● Place the breasts onto the centre of warm plates, with a little sauce, garnished with segments of orange and fresh tarragon leaves. Sprinkle the supreme with fresh strips of orange rind.

Serve with fresh noodles or on a bed of wild rice.

Malahide Roast Chicken with Mint & Garlic

*T*his coating recipe was given to me by Salvatore Palminteri, (Terry to his friends), a friend who lives in Malahide, Co.Dublin, who once owned a restaurant in Bolton. He got the recipe from an Englishman in Ireland, who came from Durham. Not that complicated really!
Bake some parsnips and carrots with the chicken at the same time and serve this with jacket potatoes and sour cream, topped with freshly snipped chives.

— Method —

- Pre-heat the oven gas 6/400f/200c.

- Place all the ingredients into a pestle and mortar and blend them. Or place them into a liquidizer and thoroughly blend.

- Place the mixture into the fridge for 4 hours and allow it to mature.

- Place the chicken in a roasting tin and coat generously with the mint and garlic coating. Mill fresh black pepper over the chicken, place in the lower end of the oven and cook for about 90 minutes, basting every 20 minutes with the coating.

Bradshawgate, Bolton.

— INGREDIENTS —

1 large chicken, cleaned, oven ready

3 sprigs fresh mint

4 cloves garlic

$^1/_2$ teaspoon salt

1 teaspoon freshly milled black pepper

4 tablespoons lemon juice

4 tablespoons olive oil

freshly milled black pepper

For the Oven
3 large parsnips, peeled and chopped

4 large carrots, peeled and sliced

4 large jacket potatoes

150g/5floz thick sour cream

1 bunch of freshly snipped chives

MATT'S MUSTARD BAKED CHICKEN

I think one of the reasons I eat so much chicken, is because my young son Matthew banned veal and other meats from our dining table. He loves baby lambs (so lamb's out), he saw a film called *Babe* on pigs (so they are out), *Watership Down* (so rabbit's out), *Bambi* (yes you guessed it), If anyone out there makes a film about a chicken, they are banned from my company. Matt is nearly 15, so he is not allowed to follow me around my favourite restaurants, where I meet all my friends like Babe, Bambi and Thumper!

— INGREDIENTS —

8 chicken pieces
(approx 100g/4oz each)

50g/2oz butter, melted

4 tablespoons mild mustard

2 tablespoons lemon juice

1 tablespoon brown sugar

1 teaspoon paprika

salt

freshly milled black pepper

3 tablespoons poppy seeds

— METHOD —

● PRE-HEAT the oven gas 6/400f/200c.

● Place the chicken pieces, smooth side down, into a large ovenproof dish.

● Place all the ingredients except the poppy seeds into a large bowl and blend them thoroughly.

● Using a pastry brush, paint the mixture onto the surface of the chicken pieces and bake in the centre of the oven for 15 minutes.

● With an oven cloth, remove the baking tray and carefully turn over the chicken pieces, coating the top side of the chicken again. Sprinkle the chicken pieces with poppy seeds and return to the oven for a further 15 minutes.

● Arrange the pieces onto a serving dish, pour over the juices and serve with a fresh, crisp tomato and sweetcorn salad.

CHICKEN SUPREME FILLED WITH TIGER PRAWNS

*T*his is not your average hot or cold recipe. I use this at buffets, served on a bed of shredded vegetables and beetroot mayonnaise in summer. In winter I serve this on a sesame bun with buttered leeks. A modern version of an old Cornish recipe.

— METHOD —

- Place each supreme onto a piece of plastic, cover the supreme and flatten it with a rolling pin until you can nearly see through it.

- Place the large leaves of blanched spinach onto the supreme, then a slice of ham, topped with another layer of spinach. Place 3 to 4 large prawns onto each supreme. Fold the pointed end of the supreme over the prawns and then fold over again to form a parcel.

- Wrap each supreme in a large piece of cling film and steam them or poach them in boiling water for 12 minutes.

- Meanwhile, melt the butter in a large frying pan and quickly fry the shredded leeks and carrots for 3 minutes. Remove the vegetables with a slotted spoon onto the centre of a large serving dish and keep warm. Gently dab of the excess butter with a paper kitchen towel.

- Place the mayonnaise and 1 beetroot into a blender and puree until very smooth. Pass the mayonnaise through a fine sieve and pour around the vegetables.

- Cut the remaining beetroot into diamond shapes and place them neatly around the mayonnaise.

- Remove the cling film from the chicken cut the supremes with a very sharp knife, into neat thin slices, and arrange onto the vegetables.

— INGREDIENTS —

4 x 200g/7oz chicken supremes, fat removed and bone left in, trimmed

100g/4oz large spinach leaves, blanched in hot salted water, stems removed

4 wafer thin slices of York ham

12 to 16 very large, raw tiger prawns, shells removed

50g/2oz butter

3 leeks, cleaned and shredded

1 large carrot, peeled and grated

150ml/5floz thick mayonnaise

2 large beetroot, cooked
(see vegetables chapter 7)

SUSSEX HOUGHED CHICKEN BREASTS

*T*he word Hough or Huffed means, "wrapped in a blanket", wrapped in pastry, using a very old method, which was used by Elizabeth Raffald in 1769.
This is a pastry version of a famous Northern recipe called *Hindle Wakes,* the stuffing is exactly the same.

— INGREDIENTS —

4 x 175g/6oz chicken breasts

450g/1lb suet crust pastry,
(see recipe on page 125)

THE FILLING
100g/4oz apple, peeled cored
and chopped

1 large onion, peeled and
chopped

100g/4oz dried prunes, stoned
and chopped

50g/2oz white breadcrumbs

1 tablespoon port

salt

freshly milled black pepper

1 large egg, beaten

— METHOD —

● PRE-HEAT the oven to gas 6/400f/200c.

● Place all the filling ingredients into a bowl, reserving a little of the egg. Blend them thoroughly.

● Make a small pocket into each chicken breast, filling them generously with the mixture.

● Roll out the pastry on a floured board. Divide the pastry into four and wrap the pastry around each chicken breast to make a parcel (pasty) shape.

● Brush the top of the pastry with the leftover beaten egg. Place them onto a lightly greased baking sheet and bake in the centre of the oven for 30-35 minutes.

ROAST GROUSE WITH BACON & DRIPPING TRIANGLES

ne in every five grand houses through out Great Britain and Ireland would have had this recipe served during the cold winter nights. Taken from my *Ultimate Game Cookbook* published by Piatkus.

— METHOD —

- PRE-HEAT the oven to gas 6/200c/400f.

- Heat the butter in a saucepan, add the lemon juice, redcurrants or cranberries and a sprinkle of salt and freshly milled black pepper. Cook for 1 minute and allow to cool.

- Fill the cavities of each bird with the currants and juice, seasoning the birds all over with salt and freshly milled black pepper.

- Wrap 2 slices of streaky bacon over each breast. Sprinkle with thyme.

- Wrap each bird in some greased foil and place them breast down in a roasting tin. Roast for 15 minutes, remove the foil and roast for a further 10 minutes.

- Heat the dripping in a frying pan and fry the bread triangles on both sides until golden brown.

- Arrange the triangles onto a large serving plate and place the grouse onto the dripping triangles.

— INGREDIENTS —

50g/2oz butter

4 oven ready grouse

juice of 1 lemon

225g/8oz red currants or cranberries

salt

freshly milled black pepper

8 rashers streaky bacon

thyme

50g/2oz beef dripping

2 slices bread cut into triangles

NELSON'S BREAST OF CHICKEN COOKED IN PORT & LEMON WITH A RUM & RAISIN SAUCE

A combination of foods used on the Tall Ships, which would have been served on Nelson's flagship HMS Victory. I devised my idea for this tribute, when the Tall Ships came through Ireland and Liverpool.

— INGREDIENTS —

4 x 175g/6oz chicken breast fillet

50g/2oz butter

2 lemons, juice and zest

3 tablespoons port

1 tablespoon white wine

150g/5oz raisins

150ml/¼ pint of sour cream

4 tablespoons dark rum

salt

freshly milled black pepper

— METHOD —

● Cut the breast fillets into thin slices, each weighing 25g/1oz, giving 6 per serving.

● Heat the butter in a frying pan, add the chicken and cook gently for 6 minutes, turning frequently until the meat is lightly coloured.

● Add the lemon and port and cook for a further 5 minutes.

● Remove from the pan, arrange in a round spiral shape on a large serving plate and keep warm.

● With the juices from the chicken in the pan, return the pan to the heat. Add the wine and raisins, simmer for 2 minutes.

● Season with salt and freshly milled black pepper, add the dark rum and cook for a further 3 minutes. Finally add the cream and reduce by half. Pour the sauce into the centre of the chicken breast spiral and serve immediately with buttered asparagus.

SUFFOLK BREAST OF TURKEY FILLED WITH LEEKS & CRANBERRIES

The Suffolk and Norfolk turkey and cranberries are a combination of meat and fruit put together in the seventeenth century, to rival the peacock. The use of chestnuts for the stuffing was introduced to the British public by Mrs Raffald and Mrs Glasse around 1730.

When you read the recipe below, you will also see how the chipolata wrapped in bacon, came to being. If you do attempt the Chestnut Sauce and Stuffing recipe, cut an X into the chestnuts on the flat side before roasting. Then the skins will come off quite easily.

From *The Art of Cookery Made Plain & Easy* by Mrs Glasse, 1747.

CHESTNUT SAUCE AND STUFFING

Roast and skin 1½lb of chestnuts for the stuffing and allow about as many for the sauce. Stuff the turkey's crop with chicken forcemeat. Fill the body with the peeled, roasted chestnuts, salt, pepper and about 8oz (225g) butter. Roast the turkey as usual.

For the sauce simmer some roasted peeled chestnuts in ½pint of good stock, when they are tender thicken the stock with a nut of butter rolled in flour, stirring it in till smooth and free of lumps. Add diced fried gammon and small fried sausages, cut in slices, just before it is served.

— METHOD —

- Pre-heat the oven to gas 6/200c/400f.

- Sauté the chopped shallots in the butter, add the leeks and cook for 2 minutes. Then add the cranberries, season and cook for a further minute. Finally add the chervil. Blend completely and allow to cool.

- Slice the breasts inwards to make a pocket, fill the pockets with the stuffing.

- Butter the breasts, wrap them in foil and cook in the oven for 30 minutes. While they are cooking make the sauce.

— INGREDIENTS —

STUFFING

2 x 450g/1lb turkey breasts

6 shallots, peeled and finely chopped

50g/2oz butter

175g/6oz leeks, thinly sliced

175g/6oz cooked cranberries

1 tablespoon chervil

SUFFOLK BREAST OF CHICKEN - SAUCE

— INGREDIENTS —

25g/1oz butter

2 shallots, chopped

150ml ¼ pint chicken stock

175g/6oz fresh Cranberries

150ml/¼ pint of white wine

150ml/¼ pint fromage frais

1 tablespoon cherry brandy

salt

freshly milled black pepper

— METHOD —

● Melt the butter in a saucepan and cook the shallots and cranberries in the butter for 3 minutes.

● Add the white wine and chicken stock and reduce by at least ¾. Add the fromage frais and cherry brandy, season and reduce by half.

Serve this sauce in a sauceboat, garnished with fresh cranberries.

Felixstowe Beach, Suffolk, 1899.

ROAST GOOSE WITH SAGE, ONION & LIME STUFFING

 oose is quite expensive today and I can only really afford to have this wonderful bird roasted during the festive season. But for the cold winter Sunday dinner, served with roast potatoes, fresh green buttered beans and giblet gravy, this becomes a meal to remember.

— METHOD —

● PRE-HEAT the oven to gas 3/325f/170c.

● Prick the goose all over with a fork, rub the orange juice into the breast and season well with the salt and pepper, including the cavity.

● Melt the butter in a frying pan and gently fry the onion and goose liver for 3 minutes. Allow the mixture to cool and blend with the rest of the ingredients in a clean bowl.

● Stuff the cavity of the goose with the mixture. Truss the goose and place it onto a rack,and into a roasting tray, (allowing the fat to flow away from the goose)

● The goose must now be roasted slowly for 3 hours, 30 minutes, breast side up. Then turn the goose over onto its breast and cook for 1 hour. Pour the excess fat into a heat resistant jug.

● Turn the goose back to breast side up and cook for the final 90 minutes.

● You can now test if the goose is cooked by placing a metal meat skewer into the leg. If the juices run clear it is cooked, if you see blood, cook for a further 20 minutes until the juices run clear.

● Place the goose onto a bed of watercress, garnished with slices of fresh lime and sage leaves, allowing the goose to cool slightly before carving.

— INGREDIENTS —

4.5kg/10lb goose, cleaned and trussed

3 tablespoons orange juice

salt

freshly milled black pepper

SAGE, ONION & LIME STUFFING
50g/2oz butter

1 large onion, peeled and chopped

goose liver, finely chopped

175g/6oz Cumberland sausage meat

225g/8oz white breadcrumbs

1 teaspoon dried sage

100g/4oz lime segments, chopped

1 teaspoon finely chopped orange peel, soaked in 1 tablespoon of lime juice

salt

freshly milled black pepper

1 bunch watercress

1 lime

1 sprig of fresh sage

Breast of Wild Lincolnshire Duckling with a Raspberry & Honey Sauce

 I wrote a similar recipe for my very popular *Heartbeat Country Cookbook* which was based on the popular Yorkshire Television series starring Nick Berry.

INGREDIENTS

Serves 4

4 x 275g/10oz breast of duckling fillets, trimmed

150ml/5floz beef stock

salt

freshly milled black pepper

25g/1oz butter

25g/1oz flour

4 tablespoons honey

100g/4oz fresh or frozen raspberries

50g/2oz finely chopped carrot

50g/2oz finely chopped shallots

1 tablespoon lemon juice

1 tablespoon Worcestershire sauce

METHOD

● Trim and score the duck breasts and season them well all over.

● Put the butter into the frying pan and seal the duck breasts.

● Add the chopped carrot, lemon juice and a little of the beef stock.

● Let it simmer for one minute then add a little honey, a few raspberries and a sprinkle of flour.

● Allow it to cook for a few minutes, season with freshly ground black pepper and add the Worcestershire sauce.

● Then repeat the process starting with the beef stock and honey, allowing 3 minutes for cooking time.

● Remove the duck breast from the pan, allowing the sauce to continue simmering.

● Slice the duck breast lengthways into ½cm/¼ inch pieces.

● Pour a little of the sauce onto the serving plate, arrange the duck breast into a fan shape and decorate with fresh raspberries and a slice of lemon.

Epsom Hare Casserole

*D*uring the early sixteenth century the forests at Epsom and Sevenoaks were rampant with hare. The towns folk and villagers from that area used their pelts to make clothing. This was the most popular recipe at that time and is still quite popular today.

— Method —

- Pre-heat the oven to gas 3/325f/170c.

- Trim the bacon, cutting each rasher into 5 or 6 pieces.

- Layer the hare, bacon and vegetables in a casserole.

- Sprinkle with the herbs, seasoning well with salt and freshly milled black pepper.

- Pour over the stock and cook for 2 hours.

- Thicken the casserole with the cornflour and wine mixture and serve with red cabbage and thick crusty bread.

— INGREDIENTS —

100g/4oz rindless streaky bacon

900g/2lb hare meat off the bone, skin removed, cleaned and chopped

4 potatoes, peeled and chopped

3 onions, sliced

2 carrots, sliced

100g/4oz mushrooms, quartered

1 teaspoon thyme and parsley

salt

freshly milled black pepper

600ml/20floz/1 pint chicken stock

15 ml/1 tablespoon cornflour blended with a little wine

High Street, Epsom, 1924.

Devonshire Rabbit with Rosemary Cider Sauce

uick and simple, great if you have a slow cooker, just throw it in and leave it!

— INGREDIENTS —

8 slices of streaky bacon,
rindless

8x175g/6oz rabbit portions

8 wooden cocktail sticks

1 tablespoon wild rosemary

1 large onion, peeled and sliced

300ml/10floz dry cider

2 tablespoons honey, warm

1 tablespoon English mustard

1 teaspoon tomato puree

salt

freshly milled black pepper

1 tablespoon cornflour mixed
with 2 tablespoons of sherry

1 apple sliced

1 sprig of fresh rosemary

— Method —

● Pre-heat the oven to gas 8/450f/230c.

● Wrap bacon around each piece of rabbit, secure with a wooden cocktail stick and place the pieces into a deep buttered casserole, cook for 20 minutes. Remove the cocktail sticks.

● Place the rosemary, onion, cider, mustard, tomato, salt and freshly milled black pepper into a bowl and mix thoroughly. Pour the mixture over the rabbit and cover.

● Lower the oven to gas 2/300f/150c and cook in the centre of the oven for 90 minutes.

● Remove the rabbit and bacon to a warm serving dish, pour the sauce into a saucepan. Heat and thicken the sauce with the cornflour.

● Pour the hot sauce over the rabbit and garnish with slices of apple and rosemary.

WARWICKSHIRE VENISON STEAK WITH BLACK CHERRIES

*S*cotland is a place of true beauty and some of the finest venison comes from that area. It can also be found in Warwickshire and around the forests of this area. In the early eighteenth century, hundreds of families made a living by making handbags and cases from the deer hides. A local family, known affectionately as the *Wilkies*, also have a few deer roaming around their back yard!

Lynne and Pete Wilkinson, alas, will not let me near them while wearing my chef whites. This recipe takes 48 hours to marinade, but it sure is worth the effort.

— METHOD —

● Place the slices of venison in a large, deep tray. Add the peppercorns, cherries and juice, shallots, bacon, juniper berries, port and wine. Season well with salt and freshly milled black pepper.

● Place the venison and marinade in the fridge for 48 hours.

● Then PRE-SET the oven to gas 4/350f/180c.

● Remove the steaks from the marinade and fry them quickly in a large frying pan with the melted butter and walnut oil for 4 minutes either side.

● Place the steaks back into the marinade (reserving the butter, oil and venison juices in the pan) and bake in the oven, covered with cooking foil, for 40 minutes. Remove the steaks from the tray to a warm serving dish. Add the flour to the juices in the frying pan and cook for 4 minutes. Add the marinade and bring to the boil, then simmer for 10 minutes until the sauce is smooth.

● Pour over the venison steaks and garnish with black cherries and fresh parsley.

— INGREDIENTS —

6 x 225g/8oz slices of venison haunch, trimmed and tenderised

6 black peppercorns, crushed

275g/10oz black cherries pitted or in syrup (pitted)

12 shallots, peeled and sliced

4 rashers of streaky bacon, rind removed and chopped

8 juniper berries

4 tablespoons of port

150ml/5floz red wine

salt

freshly milled black pepper

25g/1oz butter

2 tablespoons walnut oil

25g/1oz flour

black cherries for garnish

sprigs of fresh parsley

BAGSHOT HEATH ROAST WOOD PIGEONS IN CREAM

A delicacy since Roman times and still popular in Ireland and most countries throughout the EEC. One of those quick and simple recipes. You can use grouse or pheasant should you wish to do so. This is a typical Bagshot Heath recipe, dating back to 1870. This recipe takes 24 hours.

— INGREDIENTS —

4 wood pigeons, grouse or pheasant, trussed, (oven-ready)

75g/3oz butter, warm

1 clove garlic, crushed

salt

freshly milled black pepper

25g/1oz dripping

175g/6oz wild mushrooms

12 shallots

25g/1oz plain flour

150ml/5floz brandy

300ml/10floz double cream

1 tablespoon freshly chopped parsley

— METHOD —

● Mix the butter, crushed garlic, salt and freshly milled black pepper in a bowl. Generously rub the mixture inside and out of the pigeons and leave for 24 hours in a cool place, covered.

● PRE-HEAT the oven to gas 8/450f/230c.

● Heat the dripping in a large roasting tin and quickly brown (seal) the pigeons all over, turning them with a carving or roasting fork.

● Bake in the centre of the oven for 40 minutes, basting every ten minutes.

● Take the pigeons from the baking tray and allow them to cool slightly on a wire rack.

● Place the juices into a saucepan and cook the mushrooms and shallots for 5 minutes, then sprinkle with the flour. Add the warm brandy and ignite. Add the cream and cook for 3 minutes on a very low heat, stirring all the time.

● Carefully cut the pigeons into quarters, removing as many bones as you can. Place them into a casserole dish, cover with the cream sauce and bake in the oven for a further 12 minutes on gas 3/325f/170c. Sprinkle with freshly chopped parsley.

Serve with wild rice or roast potatoes and buttered brussel sprouts.

Chapter 6

PIES & PASTIES

The Pie Man of Bath, I read this wonderful story in Florence Whites *"Good Things in England"* published by Jonathan Cape in 1932.

Around 1875 the Pie Man stood on the Boro Walls, between Cater's and Ship and Teagles, close to the pavement by Cater's. He had a brightly polished case made of tin with a tin top, standing on four legs and fitted with three tin drawers.

In one he kept meat pies, the other mince pies and the third had a small charcoal fire arrangement which kept the pies hot.

He announced his presence by shouting repeatedly and quickly *'All 'ot all ot' all ot'* about five times rapidly, (Try it and you will get the effect).

He sold them at the recognised price of the day - one penny each. But with boys, or with men who tossed with him, if they lost he took the money, if they won they had a pie. The meat pies were 2*d*, as the men generally took meat pies, but if they did not choose they had mince pies which were cheaper.

He disappeared around 1893. He bought the stale pies from Fishers. By stale is meant pies more than a day old. I do not think confectioners are so particular today, but in my youth all confectionery was half price the day after the buns, tarts and pies were made.

This links up the mutton pies of Old England with the old Nursery rhyme:
Simple Simon met a pieman
going to the Fair,
Says Simple Simon to the pieman
"Let me taste your ware."

TRADITIONAL ENGLISH STEAK & KIDNEY PIE

*E*veryone's favourite and the most popular pie around, not only in the households of Great Britain but in restaurants, cafes and hotels all over the world.

Do not substitute cheap cuts of meat, use the best rump steak and ox kidney to achieve the perfect pie. Should you want to make this into a STEAK AND ALE PIE, then omit the kidney and soak the steak in 150ml/5floz beer overnight, then use the beer with the stock.

— INGREDIENTS —

Serves 6

575g/1.1/4lb rump steak

175g/6oz ox kidney

1 large onion

300ml/¹/₂ pint beef stock

25g/1oz seasoned flour

225g/8oz suet crust pastry
(recipe on page 125)

25g/1oz butter

salt & freshly milled black pepper

— METHOD —

● Trim the steak of the skin and fat and cut into 2.54cm/1 inch cubes (dice).

● Remove the fat, skin and core from the kidney and dice this quite small.

● Toss the steak and kidney into the seasoned flour.

● Into a large frying pan melt the butter and quickly seal the meat all over, adding the chopped onion and cooking for 4 minutes.

● Add the beef stock, season and simmer for a further 25 minutes.

● While the beef is simmering line a large, well-greased pudding basin with the suet crust pastry, leaving enough pastry to make a lid.

● Put the steak, kidney and stock into the basin and top with the lid, damping the edges with water to make it stick.

● Cover the basin with buttered tin foil or greaseproof paper.

● Stand the basin in a large saucepan with enough water to half cover it.

● Finally, bring the water to the boil and steam for 2 hours, making sure you top the water up so the pan will not dry.

MELTON MOWBRAY

I am convinced this became popular, not because it was a hunting pie, but because it originates from near to the area of Stilton. The art of pie making is quite simple, use fresh high quality ingredients and do as you are told! I have numerous recipes for this pie and I have a manuscript that beats them all. I have been waiting for the right cookery book to put this recipe in.

If you don't skimp on this recipe and follow it completely you will not be disappointed.

— METHOD —

● Make the stock by putting all the ingredients into a large pan and boiling gently for 2 hours or more until the stock has reduced to 300ml/half pint.

● Let it cool and skim off all the fat. Check the seasoning. Pour the stock through a fine, non-metallic sieve and place to one side.

Nottingham Street, Melton Mowbray, c.1955.

— INGREDIENTS —

AUTHOR'S REVISED RECIPE FROM 200 YEARS AGO

hot water pastry
(recipe on page 118)

PORK STOCK
pork bones

1 pig's foot

600ml/1pint water

1 large onion, peeled

1 carrot

1 bay leaf

2 sage leaves

1 sprig thyme

1 sprig marjoram

salt

6 peppercorns

Melton Mowbray - Pie Filling

— INGREDIENTS —

675g/1.1/2lb of pork shoulder,
(1 third fat), diced into very
small 5mm/¼ inch cubes,
skin and gristle removed

generous pinch salt

generous pinch white pepper

1 teaspoon essence of anchovy

1 egg, whisked for glaze

— METHOD —

● Combine all the ingredients in a bowl, with two tablespoons of the pork stock.

● Make up the hot water pastry as described for Cheshire Veal and Ham recipe, *(recipe on page 118).*

● Place the pie case onto a baking tray and put in the pork filling. Top with the pastry lid, firmly crimping the edges, being very careful not to break the pie case. Make a hole in the centre of the lid to allow the steam out during the cooking process. Bake in the lower part of the oven for 2 hours.

● 10 minutes before the cooking time is over, egg glaze the pie and return it to the oven.

● Turn the oven off without opening it and leave the pie in there to dry naturally for 1 hour.

● Reheat the jelly until just warm and pour into the hole of the pie, as much stock as the pie will hold.

● Let the pie cool wrap in cling film and refrigerate for at least 1 day.

Take one slice from the pie and hide before letting the family devour your hard work.

Lady Wilton's Bridge,
Melton Mowbray, c.1960.

Huntingdon Fidget - Apple & Pork Pie

*A*pple and Pork pie, served cold with pickles and chunks of cheese. This is a typical farmer's pie and would have been served cold with cheese and pickles.
Instead of apple, try using pears with a little Calvodos for a flavour with a difference.

— Method —

- **Pre-heat** the oven to gas 6/200c/400f.

- Mix the minced pork with the onion, wine, brandy, sage, Dijon mustard and apple and season this well with a generous pinch of salt and some fresh ground black pepper.

- Line the bottom of each pie mould with hot water pastry.

- Quarter fill the lined tin with the meat mixture and then the stuffing mixture, alternating until you have three linings of pork and two of stuffing .

- Roll out the remaining pastry, making the lid to fit the pie. Make a hole in the centre of the pie lid.

- Decorate with pastry leaves, egg glaze and bake for 35 minutes.

- Reduce the oven to gas 4/180c/350f and continue to bake for a further hour.

- Remove the pie from the oven and allow it to cool.

- Pour in some aspic jelly, made up with a little wine and pork stock.

- When the aspic has set, wrap the pie in cling film and allow it to mature for two days.

— INGREDIENTS —
Serves 6

900g/2lb rough minced pork

50g/2oz finely chopped onion

150ml/¼ pint Dry white wine

2 tablespoons brandy

½ teaspoon dried sage

1 tablespoon Dijon mustard

1 Bramley apple, peeled and grated coarsely

salt & fresh ground black pepper

Stuffing
175g/6oz packet stuffing (sage & onion)

50g/2oz freshly minced onion

50g/2oz freshly minced Bramley apple

blended with 150ml/5floz beef stock, darkened and blended with 225g/8oz black pudding, mashed(skin removed)

hot water pastry (*recipe on page 118*)

egg glaze

aspic jelly made with a little wine & pork stock

FOUR LAYER COUNTY CHEESE PIE

*T*he taste of my Three & Four Layer Cheese Pies, which I invented for a trade show, really is something else! The four colours of cheese, with a lining of spinach, fruit and onion between each layer, give a marble effect when you slice into the pie.

I suggest Red Leicester, Lancashire, Double Gloucester and Yorkshire/Wensleydale in that order for colour perfection, but you may use your favourites from all over Great Britain and Ireland.

INGREDIENTS
Serves 8 to 10

700g/1.1/2 lb shortcrust pastry
(recipe on page 135)

50g/2oz butter

450g/1lb onions, chopped

350g/12oz spinach leaf, trimmed,
blanched & chopped

225g/8oz of the following grated
cheeses, Red Leicestershire,
Lancashire, Double Gloucester and
Wensleydale

8 tablespoons apple puree

8 tablespoons gooseberry puree

8 tablespoons cranberry sauce

1 teaspoon freshly grated nutmeg

salt & freshly milled black pepper

3 teaspoons Worcestershire sauce

1 egg mixed with 1 tablespoon of
milk

METHOD

● PRE-HEAT the oven to gas 5/190c/375f.

● Roll out the pastry and use two-thirds of it to line a deep 10in/25cm ring pie tin or loose-based cake tin, greased with a little butter.

● Fry the onion in a little butter, 25g/1oz for 3 minutes. Add the spinach and cook for 2 minutes then season well with freshly milled black pepper and a little salt.

● Lay a lining of the spinach and onion on the base of the pie, then top with the Red Leicester and apple puree.

● Then add another lining of spinach and onion with the Double Gloucester and gooseberry puree on top.

● Then a layer of spinach and onion topped with Lancashire. Repeat the process with the final cheese, the Wensleydale and cranberry, with a sprinkle of grated nutmeg and the Worcestershire sauce.

● Use the remaining pastry to make the lid for the pie, sealing the edges. Decorate the top with any left over pastry trimmings, wash the top with the egg.

● Bake in the centre of the oven for 60 minutes until golden brown. Allow the pie to cool for at least 40 minutes and serve at room temperature with a glass of chilled dry cider.

IRISH CHEDDAR CHEESE 'N' ONION

*Y*ou can have hundreds of permutations to this pie. Simply add leeks for a likky pie, grilled streaky Irish bacon for a Bacon and Cheese pie or cooked minced beef for a Savoury Mince. The basis of every pie is to season the filling well before putting the lid on!

— METHOD —

- PRE-HEAT the oven to gas 7/425f/220c.

- Roll out the pastry on to a floured surface, using two thirds for the base and the rest for the topping.

- Grease and line a pie dish with the pastry.

- Melt the butter in a saucepan and gently fry the onions until they are transparent, about 4 minutes, and allow them to cool.

- Put them with the cheese and the rest of the ingredients into a large bowl and mix thoroughly.

- Place the mixture into the lined pie dish and top with the remaining pastry.

- Glaze with a little egg wash and bake in the oven for 30 minutes until golden brown.

For extra flavour add a little sliced apple or leeks.

— INGREDIENTS —

275g/10oz shortcrust pastry

25g/1oz butter

1 large onion, peeled and chopped

275g/10oz Irish Cheddar cheese

100g/4oz potatoes, cooked and diced

2 eggs, beaten with a little cream

pinch cayenne pepper

salt

1 egg for glaze

CHESHIRE VEAL & HAM PIE

*K*nown as the party pie in many pubs & Inns throughout the land. Perfect as a summer buffet party pie.

—INGREDIENTS—
Serves 8

450g/1lb minced veal

150g/5oz York ham, minced

1 tablespoon parsley, chopped

4 tablespoons cranberry jelly

grated rind of 1 lemon

2 onions, skinned, finely chopped

salt

freshly milled black pepper

HOT WATER PASTRY
150g/5oz lard

200ml/7floz hot water

350g/12oz plain flour, seasoned
with 1/2teaspoons salt

1 large egg yolk

4 eggs, hard-boiled and shelled

3 tablespoons powered aspic jelly

300ml/10floz clear apple juice
(warmed)

1.4 litre loaf tin, greased and lined
with greaseproof paper

—METHOD—

- PRE-HEAT the oven gas 4/180c/350f.

- Into a large mixing bowl put the veal, ham, parsley, cranberry jelly, lemon rind and onions. Add 1 teaspoon salt and some freshly milled black pepper, combine all the mixture and place to one side.

—HOT WATER PASTRY METHOD—

- Put the lard and water into a saucepan and heat gently until it has melted. Bring to the boil, remove from the heat and beat in the seasoned flour to form a soft dough. Beat the egg yolk into the dough, cover the dough with a damp cloth and rest it in a warm place for 15 minutes. Do not allow the dough to cool.

- Roll out the pastry and pat two-thirds of it into the base and sides of the tin, evenly distributed to make the shape for the pie filling.

- Place in half the meat, followed by the eggs down the centre, topping with the remaining meat mixture.

- Make a lid with the remaining pastry. Cover the pie and seal the edges, using any pastry trimmings to decorate the top. Make a large hole in the centre of the pie. Bake for 90 minutes and allow to cool for 3 hours.

- Make up the aspic jelly to 300ml 10 fl oz with apple juice, cool for 10 minutes, then pour the aspic through the hole in the top of the pie. Chill the pie for 2 to 3 hours, then remove the pie from the tin.

Slice with a warm carving knife and serve with pickles and a red cabbage salad.

NORFOLK TURKEY & YORK HAM PIE

A real after Christmas treat. This dish was also very popular during the Easter weekend and is now served at picnics and summer fetes. Norfolk is very well known for its turkeys and throughout Easter and Christmas the farmers would march them to London ready for the festivities.

— METHOD —

- PRE-HEAT the oven to gas 6/200c/400f.

- Melt the butter in a saucepan and lightly fry the carrots, onions and ham for 5 minutes.

- Blend in the flour and cook for 1 minute. Slowly add the milk, stirring continuously until the sauce thickens and becomes smooth, then simmer for 3 minutes.

- Add the chicken and cream, seasoning with salt and freshly milled black pepper.

- Should you wish at this stage to sprinkle over your favourite herb, then do so. I like to use fresh tarragon here to give it that sweet smell when you cut into the pie.

- Pour the chicken mixture into a 1.1litre/2 pint pie dish.

- Roll out the puff pastry to form a lid to fit the pie dish, sealing well and brushing the top with a little milk.

- Bake for 25-30 minutes until golden brown and serve with buttered broccoli and new mint potatoes.

— INGREDIENTS —

Serves 6

25g/1oz butter

2 carrots, diced

10 button onions, skinned

225g/8oz York ham, shredded

25g/1oz plain wholemeal flour

450ml/15floz milk

450g/1lb turkey meat, cut into strips

2 tablespoons double cream

salt

freshly milled black pepper

1 teaspoon freshly chopped tarragon or your favourite herb

275g/10oz puff pastry
(see recipe on page 135)

CUMBERLAND BACON & EGG PIE

*O*ne of those recipes that every county would have their own versions of. Avril Cooper-English, lives in Staveley near Kendal in Cumbria and her cooking is always memorable. Her husband Colin Cooper-English, is the well known creator of very special ice creams, that earned him a title and rossette in Henrietta Green's BBC Four, Food programme, *Food Lovers Guide to Britain 96/97.*

— INGREDIENTS —

225g/8oz Shortcrust pastry
(see recipe on page 135)

175g/6oz streaky bacon, rindless

5 large eggs

4 tablespoons double cream

generous pinch freshly grated nutmeg

salt

freshly milled black pepper

1 egg to glaze

— METHOD —

● PRE-HEAT the oven to gas 7/425f/220c.

● Roll out the pastry, dividing it into 150g/5oz for the base and the rest for the top.

● Grease and line a deep ovenproof pie dish with the 150g/5oz shortcrust.

● Grill the bacon until crisp, then cut it into 3cm/1inch pieces and scatter around the base of the pie. Break the eggs into the pie, leaving them completely whole and pour over the double cream.

● Season well with the nutmeg, salt and freshly milled black pepper.

● Roll out the rest of the pastry, moisten the edges of the pie and cover with the pastry.

● Press the edges together firmly, decorate the top with little leaf effects with the trimmings from the pastry, egg glaze and bake in the centre of the oven for 30 minutes, until golden brown.

Another version of this uses, Cumberland sausage cut into pieces, grilled and repeat the same process.

Castle Dairy, Kendal, Cumbria.

MAKENTIE CHICKEN & BROCCOLI PIE

I spent some of the best years of my life developing pies for a famous Northern pie manufacturers; this recipe is from my home village of Newburgh in North West Lancashire. In Wales they use leeks instead of broccoli and in Ireland they use potatoes.

The only way to get results from this type of pie is to have a shortcrust base with a puff pastry topping.

— INGREDIENTS —

50g/2oz butter

2 carrots, diced very fine

8 shallots, skinned and sliced

100g/4oz button mushrooms

25g/1oz plain flour

300ml/10floz fresh milk

150ml/5floz double cream

450g/1lb chicken breast, cooked and diced

175g/6oz broccoli florets, blanched

50g/2oz Cheddar cheese, grated

salt & freshly milled black pepper

175g/6oz shortcrust pastry for the base and 100g/4oz puff pastry for the top, *(recipes on page 135)*

1 egg for glazing

— METHOD —

● PRE-HEAT the oven to gas 6/400f/200c.

● Melt the butter in a large saucepan and gently fry the carrots, shallots and button mushrooms for about 10 minutes, stirring with a wooden spoon occasionally.

● Add the flour and cook for a further 2 minutes. Gradually add the warm milk and cream, stirring continuously until l the sauce becomes thick and creamy, simmering for 2 minutes.

● Add the chicken, broccoli and grated cheese to the sauce, seasoning well with salt and freshly milled black pepper and allow the mixture to cool.

● Roll out the short pastry base and line a greased ovenproof pie dish. Pour in the cool mixture top with puff pastry and bake in the centre of the oven for 30 minutes.

Serve this sumptuous pie with baked parsnips and creamed potatoes to soak up the very creamy sauce.

Scots Small Mutton Pies - Cold Lamb & Apricot Pie

*C*ommonly known in Scotland as Small Mutton pies, praised by Dr Johnson and a favourite of Queen Victoria. A recipe that can be made into a pasty, should you wish to save time. Excellent with red velvet beetroot or red cabbage.

— Method —

● Into a large bowl mix all the ingredients except the boiled eggs.

● Use the method for the Cheshire Veal & Ham Pie, *(on page 118),* to make up the pastry. Then follow the same process using the lamb and apricot mixture in place of the Veal and Ham.

Castle & Loch Ranza, Arran, c.1890.

— INGREDIENTS —

Serves 6

450g/1lb lean minced lamb

225g/8oz minced bacon

225g/8oz chopped apricots

1 teaspoon fresh sage, finely chopped

pinch mixed herbs

1 onion, skinned, finely chopped

4 tablespoons oatmeal

2 tablespoons brandy

3 hard boiled eggs, shelled

PASTRY & ASPIC
(see Cheshire Veal and Ham Pie, page 118)

GROUSE PIE

n Scotland and Yorkshire grouse pie is always served with fried bread and rowan jelly. True to form of a good chef I have combined these ingredients into this truly traditional Grouse Pie.

INGREDIENTS

Serves 4-6

1 tablespoon cooking oil

25g/1oz butter

1lb/16oz grouse meat

salt

freshly milled black pepper

6 slices rindless streaky bacon, finely chopped

8 shallots, peeled and sliced

1 small carrot, diced

85ml/3floz red wine

150ml/5floz chicken stock

2 tablespoons double cream

5 tablespoons rowan jelly
(see recipe on page 224)

2 tablespoons fresh parsley

275g/10oz puff pastry
(see recipe on page 135)

METHOD

● PRE-HEAT the oven to gas 6/200c/400f.

● Melt the butter with the cooking oil in a large saucepan, add the grouse meat and seal it all over. Season with salt and pepper, and simmer for 3 minutes. Add the bacon, shallots and carrot, stirring briskly for a further 3 minutes.

● Add the wine and chicken stock, bring to the boil and simmer for 25 minutes on a low heat, reducing the stock by at least $^1/_3$rd.

● Allow the grouse and sauce to cool slightly and blend in the double cream and rowan jelly.

● Roll out the pastry to fit a 1.1 litre/2 pint pie dish.

● Place the mixture into the pie dish, sprinkle with freshly chopped parsley and place on the puff pastry lid. Wash the top with a little milk and bake in the centre of the oven for 25 minutes.

● Cut 2 slices of white bread into squares and fry 25g/1oz of olive oil and 25g/1oz of butter.

● Place fried bread around the finished pie and serve.

AYLESBURY GAME PIE

*T*oday you can buy the complete range of game meat from superstores and your butcher; they stock it fresh and frozen and is not difficult at all to purchase.

Traditionally, Game Pie should be made with a puff pastry crust but I am going to show you my very own short crust pastry I have invented especially for this recipe.

— METHOD —

● Gently melt the fat in a very large saucepan add the game meat and seal by cooking for 5 minutes, extracting the juices and browning the meat quickly.

● Add the mushrooms, shallots and garlic, cooking for a further 4 minutes. Sprinkle with the flour and cook for 3 minutes, slowly add the wine and beef stock. Add the rest of the ingredients, take the pan from the heat and allow to stand for 6 hours.

● Meanwhile make up the pastry by. Sift the flour into a mixing bowl and add the suet, salt and freshly milled black pepper. Blend in the butter lightly with your fingertips. When the mixture resembles fine breadcrumbs, add the water and egg, binding into a stiff dough.

● Knead the dough lightly for 4 minutes, then cover and leave in a warm place until required.

● Bring the game mix to the boil and simmer, reducing the stock by half, cooking for at least 25 minutes.

● Place the game and the sauce into a 1.1 litre/2 pint pie dish.

● Roll out the pastry and cover the pie dish, sealing all round. Coat with a little milk and bake in the centre of the oven for 50 minutes at gas 4/180c/350f.

— INGREDIENTS —

Serves 6-8

50g/2oz butter

50g/2oz dripping or lard

775g/1.1/2 lb of mixed game meat consisting of 225g/8oz of haunch of venison, rabbit and pheasant. Pure meat no gristle and all fat removed.

225g/8oz button mushrooms

225g/8oz shallots, peeled

2 cloves garlic

3 tablespoons seasoned plain flour

300ml/10floz claret

300ml/10floz good beef stock

1 onion chopped

8 juniper berries

pinch of allspice and marjoram

1 teaspoon salt

freshly milled black pepper

SUET PASTRY

175g/6oz plain flour

50g/2oz shredded suet

pinch of salt & freshly ground pepper

75g/3oz softened unsalted butter

4 tablespoons cold water, blended with 1 egg yolk

POACHERS PIE

*R*abbits are very slowly disappearing from today's menu's and it really is a loss, because the flavour and texture of rabbit meat is something that you really cannot describe until you have actually tasted it. I think Beatrix Potter has a lot to answer for! You cannot really substitute any meat other than hare for this recipe. In Sussex, rabbits are always cooked in cider and this recipe contains a little of Sussex, but more of a Devon flavour.

— INGREDIENTS —

350g/12oz shortcrust pastry
(see recipe on page 135)

450g/1lb boneless rabbit, skinned and cubed

100g/4oz York ham, diced

1 carrot, peeled and finely diced

350g/12oz sliced potatoes

1 large apple, peeled, cored and diced

12 button onions, peeled

100g/4oz button mushrooms

salt & freshly milled black pepper

1 tablespoon freshly chopped parsley

generous pinch rosemary and thyme

150ml/5floz strong dry cider

300ml/10floz chicken stock

1 large tablespoon cornflour, blended with a little cider

1 egg, beaten to glaze

— METHOD —

• PRE-HEAT the oven to gas 7/425f/220c.

• Fill a large casserole dish (about 1.7 litres/3pints) with alternate layers of rabbit, ham, carrot, potato, onions and mushroom, seasoning each layer with salt, freshly milled black pepper and the herbs.

• Fill the casserole with the stock then cover and bake in the centre of the oven for approximately 30 minutes and then thicken the stock with the cornflour.

• Roll out the pastry, place the lid onto the casserole and trim the edge, sealing the pie all round. Make a small hole in the centre of the pastry to allow the steam to come through.

• Egg wash and bake in the centre of the oven for an hour at gas 4/350f/180c.

Serve this with crusty bread and a glass of Sussex Mead.

SHEPHERDS PIE

*H*ow many arguments have I had over this pie? If I had a pint for every argument, I would own a brewery! Shepherds pie is made with lamb and Cottage Pie with beef.

I do feel that the meat must be cooked for a Shepherds Pie and that is the first stage. I have also added extra flavours, I found the original recipes very bland, including Mrs Beeton's from 1861.

For a Northern recipe it is always sprinkled with Lancashire cheese before baking.

— METHOD —

- PRE-HEAT the oven to gas 6/400f/200c.

- Melt the dripping in a large saucepan and fry the lamb for 10 minutes, add the onions, carrots and rosemary and fry for a further 5 minutes. Season with salt and pepper.

- Add the flour and cook for a further 2 minutes. Very slowly add the stock and port, finally add the Worcestershire sauce and tomato puree and cook for a further 25 minutes, stirring every 4 minutes. Blend in the peas and allow the mixture to cool.

- Place the mixture into a deep pie dish and cover with warm mashed potato, using a fork to spread the potato, ensuring every area is completely covered.

- Sprinkle with softened butter and the crumbled Lancashire cheese and bake in the centre of the oven for 20 minutes.

— INGREDIENTS —

25g/1oz beef dripping

450g/1lb roughly minced lamb

225g/8oz loin lamb, fat removed and diced

2 large onions, skinned and sliced

2 carrots, peeled and diced

a pinch of fresh rosemary

salt & freshly milled black pepper

25g/1oz plain flour

300ml/10floz lamb stock

2 tablespoons port

1 tablespoon Worcestershire sauce

1 tablespoon tomato puree

100g/4oz sweet peas

700g/1.1/2lb warm mashed potato, seasoned buttered

25g/1oz butter, softened

75g/3oz crumbly Lancashire cheese

COTTAGE PIE

— INGREDIENTS —

25g/1oz beef dripping

450g/1lb roughly minced beef

225g/8oz rump steak, diced

1 large onion, skinned and sliced

1 large carrot, peeled and diced

a pinch of fresh thyme

salt & freshly milled black pepper

25g/1oz plain flour

300ml/10floz beef stock

1 tablespoon Worcestershire sauce

1 tablespoon tomato puree

700g/1.1/2lb warm mashed potato, seasoned buttered

25g/1oz butter, softened

— METHOD —

● PRE-HEAT the oven to gas 6/400f/200c.

● Melt the dripping in a large saucepan and fry the beef for 10 minutes, add the onions, carrot and thyme, fry for a further 5 minutes and season with salt and pepper.

● Add the flour and cook for a further two minutes and very slowly add the beef stock. Finally add the Worcestershire sauce and tomato puree and cook for a further 25 minutes, stirring every 4 minutes. Allow the mixture to cool.

● Place the mixture into a deep pie dish and cover with warm mashed potato, using a fork to spread the potato ensuring every area is completely covered.

● Sprinkle with softened butter and bake in the centre of the oven for 25 minutes.

Whiteleaf Village,
Princes Risborough, c.1955.

NOBBY'S TATTIE PIE

*T*his is one of those recipes that I had passed on to me by my dad (Nobby), an ex-soldier so he loved home-cooked food! He had a very special way of cooking it. If you could put a spoon in his Tattie Pie mixture and it fell over, it was not thick enough! *'that's a dad for ya'*.

METHOD

- PRE-HEAT the oven to gas 6/200c/400f.

- Into a large saucepan, heat the dripping until it is quite hot. Add the mince and very quickly seal and brown it for 5 minutes. Add the potatoes, carrot, onion and mixed herbs, cooking for 4 minutes. Sprinkle with the flour, stir, add the peas and beef stock, bring to the boil and simmer for 15 minutes. Season with salt and freshly milled black pepper.

- Put the mixture into a 1.1 litre/2 pint pie dish. Scatter the diced black pudding over the top (this helps to thicken the pie contents during the cooking process).

- Make up the pastry as for Game Pie, cover the pie dish, sealing and crimping the pastry all around.

- Trim off any excess pastry and decorate with pastry leaves.

- Brush with milk and bake in the centre of the oven for 30-45 minutes.

INGREDIENTS

Serves 6-8

25g/1oz beef dripping

675g/1.1/2lb roughly minced beef

900g/2lb potatoes, peeled and diced

150g/5oz diced carrot

225g/8oz sliced onion

1 tablespoon mixed herbs

25g/1oz plain flour

100g/4oz marrowfat peas

300ml/10floz beef stock

salt

freshly milled black pepper

225g/8oz black pudding, skin removed and diced

Pastry as for Game Pie *(page 125)*

fresh milk, to glaze

STARGAZY PIE

*C*ornwall is not only famous for the Cornish Pasty but also for this very unusual pie using herrings. The original recipe had the heads of the herrings sticking out of the pie looking up to the stars. With a filling of boiled eggs and bacon, it was like a Cornish breakfast all in one pie!

— INGREDIENTS —

8 herrings fillets,
bone and skin removed

50g/2oz butter

25g/1 flour

150g/5floz warm milk

150g/5floz cider

1 tablespoon sherry

anchovy essence

75g/3oz Cheddar cheese,
grated

2 hard boiled eggs, chopped

175g/6oz streaky bacon,
rindless, grilled and chopped

225g/8oz shortcrust pastry
(see recipe on page 135)

1 egg to glaze

—METHOD—

● PRE-HEAT the oven gas 6/400f/200c.

● Put the herring fillets into a large saucepan and fry them gently in the butter for 4 minutes on either side. Carefully place them into the bottom of a pie dish.

● Add the flour to the butter in the frying pan and cook for 1 minute. Slowly blend in the warm milk and cider to make a smooth sauce. Add the sherry and anchovy essence, cooking for a further 2 minutes, stirring constantly.

● Cover the herring fillets with the cheese, boiled egg and chopped streaky bacon. Pour over just enough of the sauce to cover the herrings.

● Roll out the pastry and cover the pie dish, brush with the beaten egg and bake in the centre of the oven for 30 minutes.

"*OGGIE*" - CORNISH PASTY

ary Evelyn (Florence White) wrote *Good Things In England* in 1932, and suggested someone should write a book about *The Pyes of Olde England*. I feel that this chapter will cover most of it and it is through her work, that I relate my experiences. The Cornish pasty is one of the few forms of English cookery that conserves all the value of the food. It contains meat, turnip and onion, with the pastry joined at the side. The ultimate portable lunch for the working men of Cornwall.

It is very important here that the meat and vegetables are diced very small, about 1cm x 1cm/$^1/_2$ inch square. A recipe from 1922, St.Ives, uses 100g/$^1/_4$ lb of calves liver, finely chopped and blended with the steak. Having tasted many a Cornish pasty, the one with the most flavour, which I have seen produced at first hand, is Ginsters.

'*There is no love sincerer than the love of food*' Bernard Shaw
"*Pastry rolled out like a plate,*
Piled with turmut, tates and mate,
Doubled up, and baked like fate,
That's a Cornish pasty,"

— METHOD —

● PRE-HEAT the oven to gas 7/425f/220c.

● Heat the dripping in a large saucepan, add the meat and vegetables and cook for 8 minutes, stirring all the time with a wooden spoon. Season the mixture well and allow it to cool completely.

● Roll out the pastry to about 5mm/$^1/_4$ inch thick and cut out 4-6, 15cm/6 inch rounds.

● Put equal amounts of the mixture into the centre of each round. Dampen the edge of the rounds with beaten egg and fold each round over to make a half moon shape.

● Turn the edges round to make small turns (horns), pinching and crimping the edges to seal the pasty completely. Glaze with beaten egg and place the pasties onto a greased baking sheet.

● Bake in the centre of the oven, lowering the heat after 10 minutes to gas 4/350f/180c, for 30 minutes.

— INGREDIENTS —

450g/1lb shortcrust pastry
(*see recipe on page 135*)

25g/1oz beef dripping

350g/12oz rump steak, diced

4 potatoes, peeled and diced

1 large onion, peeled and chopped

1 large carrot, peeled and diced

100g/4oz turnip, diced

salt & freshly milled black pepper

1 tablespoon parsley

1 egg, beaten with a little milk

FORFAR BRIDIES - WELSH CHICKEN & LEEK PASTRY

*T*his is very similar to the Cornish Pasty except that it is more of a steak pasty than a Cornish. They were invented by Mr Jolly, a baker in Forfar around the 1870s. Why Bridies? Because they are a simple meal that a young bride could add to her cookery book.

Exactly the same as Cornish but omit the potato, carrot and turnip. Simply add a generous pinch of dried English mustard to the seasoning.

THE WELSH CHICKEN & LEEK PASTRY - is a variation on the Bridie. When the miners could not afford chicken sausage meat was often used. The Irish version uses diced potatoes with strong onions in place of leeks.

— INGREDIENTS —

Makes 6-8

450g/1lb chicken breast meat, roughly chopped

50g/2oz butter

4 leeks, cleaned and finely chopped

2 sprigs fresh parsley

3 tablespoons redcurrant jelly

225g/8oz potatoes, cooked and diced

salt

freshly milled black pepper

450g/1lb shortcrust pastry
(see recipe on page 135)

beaten egg and a little milk

— METHOD —

● Put the chicken meat into a frying pan with the butter, leeks and parsley. Cook and cover for 25 minutes, stirring every five minutes.

● Add the jelly and potatoes, seasoning well and allow to cool.

● Roll out the pastry to 5mm/$\frac{1}{4}$ inch in thickness and cut out 8 x 15cm/6 inch rounds.

● Place the chicken mixture into the centre of each round, dampen the edges and fold them over to make a half moon shape then pinch and crimp the edges.

● Glaze with the beaten egg and put the pasties onto a greased baking sheet.

● And bake at gas 4/180c/350f for 35 minutes.

Serve with a crisp vegetable salad.

The Summit, Snowdon, c.1887.

YORKSHIRE MINT PASTIES

*T*he ingredients for the mint pasty are very similar to that of the Eccles Cake, Chorley Cake and Newburgh Cakes of Lancashire.

I know the battle of the roses goes on in cricket, I might just start another with pasties.

— INGREDIENTS —

Serves 4

225g/8oz shortcrust pastry

25g/1oz butter

100g/4oz currants

25g/1oz mixed peel

50g/2oz mixed fruit

50g/2oz Demerara sugar

½ teaspoon mixed spice

½ teaspoon freshly grated ginger

½ teaspoon freshly grated nutmeg

3 tablespoons freshly chopped mint

— METHOD —

● PRE-HEAT the oven to gas 7/220c/425f.

● Melt the butter in a saucepan, add and blend all the ingredients and allow the mixture to simmer for 4 minutes. Then let the mixture cool.

● Roll out the pastry, then with a 15cm/6 inch cutter or saucer, cut it into rounds.

● Put a generous tablespoon of the mixture into the centre of each round. Dampen the edges and fold over to form a half moon shape then gently flatten the mixture with the palm of your hand.

● Seal the edges, brush lightly with a little milk and place them onto a greased baking sheet.

● Bake in the centre of the oven for 15-20 minutes until golden brown.

Making Good Pastries

Shortcrust Pastry

*G*ood pastry should be light in texture, it is important that you always weigh the ingredients accurately and keep all the ingredients, utensils and your clean hands as cool as possible.

— Method —

- Sift the flour and salt into a clean bowl, then gently rub in the butter and lard until the mixture resembles fine breadcrumbs.
- Add enough cold water to make a stiff dough. Press the dough together with your fingertips.
- Sprinkle with a little sifted flour, then roll the pastry out on a lightly floured surface. Use as in the recipes.

— INGREDIENTS —

350g/12oz plain flour

$^1/_2$ teaspoon salt

75g/3oz butter

75g/3oz lard

flour for rolling out

Puff Pastry

*W*hen making puff pastry, it is worth while making a large batch and freezing half of it down, because it is a long and drawn out, time consuming job. It will keep frozen for up to 3 months.

— Method —

- Sift the flour and salt into a clean mixing bowl. Gently rub in 50g/2oz of the butter. Add the lemon juice and a little cold water to make a smooth dough.
- Shape the remaining butter into a rectangle on a sheet of greaseproof paper.
- Carefully roll out the dough on a lightly floured surface to a strip a little wider than the butter and twice the size in length.
- Place the butter on of half of the pastry, gently fold over the other half, pressing the edges with the floured rolling pin.
- Leave the pastry in a cool place for 20 minutes to allow the butter to harden.
- Roll out the pastry on a lightly floured surface. It is here you must think about 1/thirds.
- Fold the bottom third up and the top third down, pressing the edges together with the rolling pin, turning the pastry so the folded edges are on the right and left of you. Roll and fold again, cover and leave in a cool place for 15 minutes. Repeat this process of rolling out six times.

The pastry is now ready for use.

— INGREDIENTS —

225g/8oz plain flour

$^1/_4$ teaspoon salt

225g/8oz butter

$^1/_2$ teaspoon lemon juice

flour for rolling

MAKING GOOD PASTRIES CONTINUED

MY MOTHERS SUET PASTRY

I suppose that nobody can bake better than their mother and everyone loves their mother. Well I also hold very close to me my mother's love and understanding of making suet pastry.

Suet should, if at all possible, be fresh and your butcher will sell it to you at any time. It should be grated on a cheese grater and seasoned with a little salt before use.

"Warm hands make a warm heart but not really good pastry" My mum, 1960's.

— INGREDIENTS —

225g/8oz self raising flour

75g/3oz butter, softened

50g/2oz freshly shredded suet

salt

freshly milled black pepper

1 egg (size 3)

1 tablespoon water

— METHOD —

● Place the flour, butter and suet into a bowl, season with a little salt and freshly milled black pepper.

● Rub together with your fingertips until the mixture resembles fine breadcrumbs.

● Mix the egg and water together, make a well in the centre of the flour mixture and pour in the egg.

● Mix together until a soft paste forms. Turn the mixture out onto a floured work surface and knead into a soft but fairly firm dough.

● Makes approx 450g/1lb suet pastry.

Deansgate, Bolton.

Chapter 7

VEGETABLES

O nly the best British and Irish cooks would recognise words like Champ, Pan Haggerty and Squeak. I have put together several famous British and Irish vegetable recipes, starting with Pan Haggerty, which is succulent layer of potatoes, Cheddar cheese and onions from the North East of England. I have also included some new healthy eating ideas for vegetarians - showing you how to make use of the redundant beetroot and some quite exciting potato recipes like *crisps!* I am very lucky to have some close friends in the vegetable business. All my beetroot is supplied by Brian Olverson at Red Velvet Beetroot in Scarisbrick near Southport and the rest of my vegetables by Oliver Kay at Rediveg in Bolton. My last visit brought me the finest Lincolnshire asparagus supplied to Rediveg by C.Wright & Son in Gedney and the finest of graded potatoes for my Pan Haggerty, which I am sure you will enjoy serving on its own or with a light lunch.

Potato Seller, London, c.1890.

PAN HAGGERTY

 true taste of Ireland and North East England, this recipe dates back to the late seventeenth century and can be served with most main course foods.

— INGREDIENTS —

450g/1lb potatoes, peeled and thinly sliced

50g/2oz beef dripping

450g/1lb onions, peeled and sliced

salt

freshly ground black pepper

175g/6oz Irish Cheddar cheese, grated

Irish brown bread & butter

— METHOD —

- Heat the dripping in a large based frying pan.

- Remove the pan from the heat and interlay the potatoes, onions and cheese, seasoning well with salt and pepper between each layer, ending with a top layer of cheese.

- Cover and cook the haggerty gently for 25 minutes.

- Uncover and brown the top of the dish under a hot grill.

- Serve the dish straight from the pan with crusty brown bread and butter or with your favourite main course as a vegetable.

Women and Children on doorstep.

The Great British Potato - Game Chips

*T*here are well over a dozen different varieties of potato grown commercially in Great Britain, thanks to Thomas Herriot's voyage to the Americas with Sir Walter Raleigh. King Edward and Majestic in England, Kerr's Pink, Redskin and Golden Wonder in Scotland are the maincrop and principal varieties of potato which are harvested from early October.

Early potatoes should be purchased in small quantities as they very quickly lose their crisp flavour. There are several varieties which include Red Craigs Royal, Maris Peer, Home Guard and Arran Pilot. The most famous of potatoes are without doubt the King Edward and the Maris Piper. My favourite potato is the Royal potato, the Jersey Royal.

Crisps are now one of the biggest selling food items around the world; the aristocrats today would not touch them, unless they were served using their proper title and with the right food.

No, it is not Salt & Linekar or Cheese & Owen flavoured Walkers, they are known as *Game Chips*. The potatoes must be so thin that you can see through them, you can do this by using a mandolin, the thin line on a cheese grater or a food processor.

— Method —

● Soak the thinly sliced potatoes in cold water for 40 minutes to remove the excess potato starch. Dry them thoroughly in a clean tea towel, or paper kitchen towel.

● Heat the oil in a deep chip frying pan. Place half the potatoes into the frying basket. When it is smoking, carefully lower the potatoes into the hot oil and cook for 4 to 5 minutes until golden brown, shaking the basket every minute so they do not stick together.

● Drain them onto a paper kitchen towel, salt and place under the grill for a few seconds to dry them out.

● Repeat the process with the rest of the potatoes.

— INGREDIENTS —

450g/1lb peeled and very thinly sliced potatoes

peanut oil for deep frying

sea salt

BUBBLE & SQUEAK - VEGETABLE FILLED CAKES (VEGETARIAN DELIGHT)

*F*rom my book *The Golden Age Of Cookery*, 1983.

Bubble & squeak, a fry up, was a favourite during the eighteenth century. The earliest use of the term so far discovered was in a Burlesque translation of *Homer*, written by my namesake, Thomas Bridges, in 1767. It was also known in Devon as Devonshire Stew, around 1837.

We therefore cook'd him up a dish of lean bull-beef with cabbage fried,
and a full pot of beer beside:
Bubble they call this dish, and squeak; Our taylors dine on't thrice a week.

I am sure, after you have seen me make these very tasty Bubble & Squeak Cakes, you will be making them for dinner parties and for the family every week. I came up with this idea after talking to several vegetarians who got bored with the very mundane foods offered to them. The choice of filling is your own, the flavour of the Bubble and Squeak with your surprise centre makes this one of the next up and coming vegetarian delights.

INGREDIENTS

25ml/1floz cooking oil

1 medium onion, skinned and finely chopped

450g/1lb potatoes, cooked and mashed

225g/cooked cabbage, finely chopped

salt & freshly milled black pepper

sifted plain flour

1 egg & a little milk, whisked together

sesame seeds

poppy seeds

25g/1oz dripping or lard

METHOD

● Heat the oil in a large frying pan, and add the chopped onion. Cook for 3 minutes then add the cabbage and cook for a further 3 minutes. Finally add the potatoes, season with salt and pepper and fry over a medium heat for a further 10 minutes. Blend the mixture during the cooking process.

● Remove the mixture from the pan into a clean glass bowl and allow to cool.

● Flour a cutting board and your hands.

● Take about 50g/2oz of the mixture, roll into a ball and then flatten it like a pancake.

● Put your favourite cooked vegetable onto the mixture and fold it over, hiding the vegetable in the centre of the mixture.

● Flatten and shape the mixture into little rounds. Flour and egg wash, coat with some sesame or poppy seeds then fry in a little hot dripping until golden brown, about 3 minutes either side.

OTHER SUGGESTED FILLINGS FOR THE BUBBLE & SQUEAK CAKES

APPLE, FENNEL, MUSHROOMS, AVOCADO, FRUITS, NUTS, GREEN BEANS, HERBS, PARSNIP, BEETROOT, KIDNEY BEANS, BEAN SPROUTS, BROCCOLI, LEEKS, SPINACH, GRATED CARROT, LENTILS, STIR-FRY VEGETABLES, CHEESE, MACARONI, SWEET POTATO, CHILLI, MANGETOUT, TOFU, RICE, EGGS, PASTA, BAKED BEANS, ARTICHOKES, SWEET & SOUR VEGETABLES

● Try brown rice or whole meal pasta, foods that are high in fibre. School children love them with tinned beans, again high in fibre, low in fats, an ideal combination.

● The vegetables must be cooked El-Dente (crisp) and allowed to cool before putting them into the centre of the Bubble & Squeak Cakes.

● Try mixing any herbs, spices, pulses, nuts, grains, fruits or berries with any of the above. Remember you should Live to Eat and NOT, Eat to Live. Enjoy. . .

● The word Al or El Dente simply means not to be over-cooked in vegetable terms; to be crisp to the bite, but not raw.

Still Life of Vegetables.

CHAMP & COLCANNON

hamp is a dish from the North of Ireland.
It is a straight forward Irish recipe, served as a dish by itself.

INGREDIENTS

450/1lb Irish Potatoes

4 tablespoons hot milk

1 onion, chopped

25g/1oz butter

100g/4oz peas

salt &pepper

METHOD

- Boil 450g/1lb of Irish potatoes and mash them with 4 tablespoons hot milk and 1 onion, chopped and fried in 25g/1oz butter.

- Season well with salt and freshly milled pepper.

- Serve with 100g/4oz cooked peas blended with a little butter and you're a *CHAMP*.

olcannon - Simple and quick, this dish is usually served with Irish ham or bacon ribs.

INGREDIENTS

1 large onion or 6 scallions, finely chopped

50g/2oz best Irish butter

150ml/5floz fresh, creamy milk

450g/1lb cooked, mashed potato

225g/8oz cooked Savoy cabbage, finely chopped

lo-salt

freshly milled black pepper

METHOD

- Fry the onion with the butter for three minutes, add the milk and mashed potato, blending thoroughly and cooking for a further 3 minutes.

- Add the chopped cabbage, blend and cook for 5 minutes, seasoning well with the lo-salt and freshly milled black pepper.

Olivers Spinach & Wild Mushroom Bake

*O*ne of the tastiest vegetarian dishes. Always check and recheck the seasoning in vegetables, it is most important. Remember you can add a little more seasoning to a recipe but you cannot take it out once it has been added!

— Method —

- Pre-heat the oven gas 6/400f/200c.

- Trim and clean the mushrooms.

- Melt 50g of the butter in a saucepan and gently fry the garlic, shallots and wild mushrooms for 3 minutes.

- Blend in the spinach, Cheddar cheese, nutmeg and basil. Season well with salt and freshly ground black pepper and place to one side.

- In another saucepan melt the remaining margarine, add the flour and cook for 1 minute. Slowly add the hot milk, whisking until smooth. Add 25g of the Cheshire cheese, season with salt and freshly ground black pepper.

- Spread half the mushroom and spinach mixture onto the bottom of a lightly greased ovenproof dish.

- Top with a layer of lasagne, then half the white sauce.

- Repeat the process. Sprinkle with Cheshire cheese and cook in the oven for 30 minutes until golden brown.

Serve with crusty bread.

— INGREDIENTS —

100g/4oz butter

225g/8oz wild mushrooms

100g/4oz shallots

450g/1lb spinach, cooked, drained and finely chopped

225g/8oz Irish Cheddar cheese

5ml/1 teaspoon basil

2 cloves garlic

1.25 ml/$^1/_4$ teaspoon freshly grated nutmeg

salt

freshly ground black pepper

50g/plain flour

600ml/1 pint hot milk

8 sheets lasagne pasta, cooked and drained

50g/2oz Cheshire cheese

VEGETABLE CASSEROLE

This very well known British stew is also now known as the classical French vegetable stew, *"Ratatouille"*, introduced to me several years ago when I was a very young chef, learning the art of vegetable cookery. I was taught to cook it for 40 to 45 minutes and found that it overcooked and became very sloppy.

An ideal vegetarian dish when placed inside an aubergine, topped with grated cheese and then oven baked.

— INGREDIENTS —

120ml/4floz olive oil

2 large aubergines

3 large courgettes

1 large onion

6 large tomatoes

1 large green pepper

1 large red pepper

3 cloves garlic

50g/2oz tomato puree

sea salt

freshly milled black pepper

1/2 teaspoon/2.5ml basil

— METHOD —

● Cut the ends off the aubergines and courgettes, wash them thoroughly and dry them.

● Cut them into 2.5cm/1 inch chunks. To remove the bitter juices from the aubergine, sprinkle them with salt and place them in a colander for 20 minutes. Rinse them before cooking.

● Scald the tomatoes, remove the skins and chop them roughly.

● Wash the peppers, remove the white inner ribs and all the seeds and cut them into 2.5cm/1inch dice shapes. Peel and coarsely chop the garlic and onion.

● Heat the olive oil in a large saucepan and fry the onion and garlic for 3 minutes.

● Stir in the remaining vegetables, tomato puree and basil, season well, cover and simmer for 20 minutes, stirring every 5 minutes.

Serve with or in baked jacket potatoes topped with a little sour cream.

POTATO PANCAKE & POTATO CAKES

*C*hefs all over England have gone potato pancake mad, but they call it *Swiss Rosti* and use shredded raw potatoes. This recipe dates back to Edwardian cookery. Rosa Lewis used the same method to make Potato Baskets, into which she placed minted peas or devilled whitebait. The Irish call this *Boxty* and serve it with bacon and white pudding.

— POTATO PANCAKE METHOD—

● Boil the potatoes in their skins for 10 minutes, then plunge them into cold water and leave them to go completely cold for at least 1 hour.

● Then skin the potatoes and grate them with a coarse grater. Melt the butter in a large saucepan. Put the grated potato in small pancake shaped heaps and sprinkle with salt, pepper and freshly grated nutmeg. Cook for 12 minutes. As the potatoes brown, turn them over and repeat the process.

● Press down gently on the potato mixture, to release any excess fat and remove onto a warm serving plate.

— POTATO CAKES METHOD—

● Blend the potato, onion and egg with just enough flour to stop the cakes becoming too moist.

● Shape into little flat cakes on a floured board.

● Put the dripping into a frying pan. When the dripping is hot add the cakes, cooking for 3 minutes either side, until they are golden brown.

— INGREDIENTS —
POTATO PANCAKES
4 large jacket potatoes

75g/3oz butter

salt

freshly milled black pepper

freshly grated nutmeg

— INGREDIENTS —
POTATO CAKES
45g/1lb cooked potato, mashed and seasoned

25g/1oz finely chopped onion

1 egg beaten with 2 teaspoons fresh milk

plain flour

50g/2oz dripping

WELSH POTATO & ONION BAKE

*I*t's the Caerphilly Cheese that gives this bake the unique flavour, no other cheese will do! Use it very Caer-phill-y.

— INGREDIENTS —

6 large baking potatoes, peeled and finely sliced

2 large onions, peeled and finely sliced

100g/4oz Caerphilly cheese, grated

100g/4oz leeks, finely cut

freshly milled black pepper

salt

150ml/5floz milk, blended with 1 egg

4 tablespoons vegetable stock

— METHOD —

● PRE-HEAT the oven to gas 6/400f/200c.

● In a large, shallow, ovenproof dish, alternate the potatoes, onion, cheese and leeks, seasoning each layer. Pour over the milk, egg and vegetable stock.

● Cover and bake in the centre of the oven for 40 minutes, remove the cover and bake for a further 10 minutes.

Caerphilly Castle, 1893.

SALFORD THATCH

*T*his recipe was usually served at tea-time with sausages, egg and tomatoes. I have a feeling this is a transformation of Elizabeth Raffald's recipe from 1769. Also look at the very close similarity to the *Swiss Rosti*. It does make me think, that some Swiss gentleman came over here in the 1700's and went back and created their own recipe, I wonder what they called it?

— METHOD —

● Blend all the ingredients, except the dripping, together in a large bowl.

● Melt the dripping in a large saucepan, when it is hot, spread the mixture evenly over the base of the pan.

● Cook gently until crisp and brown on the base and completely set on the top. Carefully place a plate over the frying pan and turn out onto the plate.

● Place the uncooked side back into the pan and cook until crisp and brown.

● Place onto a large, warm serving plate, cut into wedges and serve.

— INGREDIENTS —

450g/1lb grated raw potato

225g/8oz streaky bacon, rindless, chopped

50g/2oz plain flour, seasoned

3 large eggs, beaten with 4 tablespoons single cream

25g/1oz dripping

— CHEF'S ALTERNATIVE TIP —
Try the same method using CARROT &
PARSNIP, 225g/8oz of each, grated and
blanched in butter for 4 minutes.

GEDNEY ASPARAGUS PANCAKES

*G*edney in Lincolnshire have some of the finest asparagus in Great Britain, along with Formby. This pancake can be filled with your favourite vegetables as long as they are cooked before hand. One of my favourites is shredded parsnips with a tablespoon of mustard.

Try shredded leek with mushroom, or beetroot and diced potato, the list is endless and is very much based on the idea of my Bubble & Squeak recipe.

— INGREDIENTS —

25g/1oz butter

Lincolnshire Asparagus spears, cooked (el dente)

100g/4oz red pepper, finely diced

150ml/5floz double cream

25g/1oz plain flour

salt

4 egg yolks

freshly milled black pepper

25g/1oz butter with 4 tablespoons olive oil

— METHOD —

● Slice the asparagus into small pieces.

● Gently cook the peppers in the 25g/1oz butter for 4 minutes. Drain and dry with paper kitchen towel. Place the peppers with the asparagus into a clean bowl.

● Whisk the cream, flour, salt and egg yolks together. When smooth add the asparagus and peppers, seasoning well with freshly milled black pepper.

● Heat the butter and oil in a large frying pan and drop tablespoons of the mixture into the pan. Fry until golden brown on both sides, using all the mixture.

Doughty Quay, Boston, 1890.

CREAMED MUSHROOMS

One of nature's foods, but you must have a knowledge of mushrooms, when mushroom picking. Never over cook mushrooms, they lose their flavour very quickly. The people of Wales serve these with toast.

TO RAGOO MUSHROOMS : ELIZABETH RAFFALD, 1769.

Take large mushrooms, peel and take out the inside, broil them in a gridiron, when the outside is brown put them into a tossing pan, with as much water as will cover them ,let them stand for ten minutes, then put to them a spoonful of white wine, the same of browning,a very little allegar, thicken it with flour and butter, boil it a little, lay sippets round your dish, and serve it up.

— INGREDIENTS —

50g/2oz butter

1 tablespoon olive oil or walnut oil

6 shallots, peeled and sliced

450g/1lb button mushrooms, sliced

salt

freshly milled black pepper

1 teaspoon plain flour

150ml/5floz double cream

2 tablespoons port

freshly grated nutmeg

1 tablespoon freshly chopped parsley

3 slices white bread, cut into triangles, fried in hot dripping

— METHOD —

● Heat the butter and oil in a large saucepan, add the shallots and cook for 3 minutes, then add the mushrooms and cook on a low heat for 2 minutes.

● Season with salt and freshly milled black pepper, sprinkle with a little flour and cook for 1 minute. Add the cream, port and grated nutmeg and cook for 8 minutes on a low heat.

● Sprinkle with chopped parsley and serve with crispy triangles of bread fried in dripping.

SPINACH AS A VEGETABLE
Mrs Mary Eaton, Bungay, Suffolk, 1823.
This really is an interesting recipe when you consider what she says at the end.
1. Wash and pick the spinach carefully (900g/2lb).
2. Throw it into a saucepan with a little salt (1teaspoon).
3. Set the pan on the fire (cook slowly) and shake it well.
4. When sufficiently done (4 minutes), beat up the spinach with some butter (50g/2oz) but it must be sent to the table pretty dry. A little cream is an improvement (4tablespoons)

N.B. It would look well, if pressed into a tin mould in the form of a large loaf, which is now obtainable (in 1823).

BRAISED FENNEL

I have been using this aniseed flavoured vegetable on a regular basis over the last few years. It is one of those that you can use in salads and is quite exciting to use in baking, to give fish and meat that extra punch.

—METHOD—

- PRE-HEAT the oven to gas 4/350f/180c.

- Carefully trim the green shoots from the tops of the fennel and trim the bases. Then gently peel off the first layer, placing to one side.

- Quarter the fennel and place them into a large saucepan with the vegetable stock and outer skins. Bring the pan to the boil and simmer for 5 minutes.

- Remove the fennel with a slotted spoon to a ovenproof casserole, discarding the outer skins.

- Bring the vegetable stock to the boil and reduce by half.

- Melt the butter and fry the chopped bacon and the shallots in a saucepan for 4 minutes, then add the flour, vegetable stock, cream and Madeira. Cook through for 3 minutes until the sauce is smooth, season well and pour over the fennel. Braise in the centre of the oven for 25 minutes.

—INGREDIENTS—

6 fennel bulbs

150ml/5floz vegetable stock

25g/1oz butter

6 slices of smoked streaky bacon, rindless

6 shallots, peeled and quartered

25g/1oz flour

100ml/3floz cream

1 tablespoon Madeira

freshly milled black pepper

SCARISBRICK RED VELVET BEETROOT & ORANGE MOULD

I created this for the Olverson Red Velvet Beetroot company who grow this wonderful vegetable in the fields at Scarisbrick near Southport and sell it all over the world. Working with Brian Olverson is always a pleasure, together we create ideas for most major supermarkets. Red Velvet Beetroot is wonderful baked with a Sunday roast, barbecued in summer or tossed in a light mustard & honey sauce for a summer salad, but for something completely different try this.

— INGREDIENTS —

450g/1lb Red Velvet cooked beetroot and finely chopped

300ml/10floz double cream

4 eggs

salt

pinch of ground rosemary

freshly milled black pepper

1 large orange, cut into segments

— METHOD —

- PRE-HEAT the oven to gas 1/275f/140c.

- Ensure that the beetroot is dry and put it with the cream into a food processor and blend thoroughly. Pass the mixture through a very fine sieve.

- Whisk the eggs briskly and add them to the beetroot mixture, add the rosemary and season well.

- Pour the mixture into a buttered pudding mould. Place the orange segments around the pudding mould, lengthways down into the beetroot mixture.

- Place the pudding basin carefully into a baking tray half filled with warm water. Cover with cooking foil and bake in the centre of the oven for 60 minutes until the beetroot mixture is firm to the touch.

- Allow the mould to cool naturally and serve warm or cold with your favourite meat or fish recipe.

CAKES & BISCUITS

Chapter 8

I have dug out recipes dating back to the fifteenth century for this section. They remind me of my grandmother baking in her little back kitchen in Bolton; whenever my mother took me to see my grandmother the smell of home-made Hovis was prominent. This choice of recipes will certainly bring a smile to your face. In the North we still have two very good bakeries, Greenhalgh's and Warburtons. Having worked with Allan Smart at Greenhalgh's and Derrick Warburton at Warby's, my experience in this section is second to none. Happy cooking. . . this section is dedicated to these very special people who put sunshine into my cookery lessons.

Fry's Chocolate Advert.

ENGLISH SCONES

*T*he word scone is believed to come from the Gaelic word "sgonn", (a large mouthful). Fruit scones have been a part of the afternoon tea and the main menu of many Country House Hotels for several years. It is very important that the flour is sifted twice with the bicarbonate of soda and that the butter is soft to the touch.

— INGREDIENTS —

225g/8oz self raising flour

1 level teaspoon
bicarbonate soda

75g/3oz soft butter

50g/2oz sultanas

50g/2oz glace cherries, roughly
chopped

50g/2oz caster sugar

1 egg

150ml/¼ pint of milk

— METHOD —

● PRESET the oven to gas 8/230c/450f.

● Into a large mixing bowl, sift the flour and bicarbonate of soda, twice. Add the softened butter and very lightly with your fingertips blend it into the flour, lifting the mixture gently all the time.

● Toss the sultanas and cherries in a little flour then add them with the sugar. Blend the milk and egg together in a cup.

● Add the milk and egg slowly to the mixture, very lightly blending with your fingertips. Save some of the egg mixture to coat the scones before baking.

● When the mix is a soft to the touch dough, place it onto a floured board and gently knead flat with the heal of your hand. Knead out the dough until 1 inch thick and cut into scones with a 2 inch pastry cutter, or cut into diamond shapes with a knife.

● Set on an ungreased baking tray and brush the tops gently with the egg and milk, making sure it does not run down the sides of the scone.

● Bake in the centre of the oven for 12 minutes until light golden brown.

ECCLES CAKE - TOM'S PERFECT PUFF PASTRY

*E*very where I go I am asked the Eccles cake story, This is a recipe which I have been hounded by bakeries across the country to re-create. People that come to my home automatically think they can smell them being made.

Eccles, Hawkshead, Banbury, Chorley, Newburgh and Coventry Godcakes all belong to the same class. They are made of short or puff pastry. The Eccles cake, like the Newburgh cake, is smaller than the Chorley cake, all are filled with a special mixture.

Here is the mother of English cookery's recipe, Elizabeth Raffald, (1733-1781), who invented the Eccles cake. For Allan Smart.

—— METHOD ——

- Sift the flour and salt into a bowl.

- Lightly rub in 50g/2oz of the butter.

- Add sufficient water and lemon juice to make a firm dough.

- Refrigerate for 40 minutes.

- Lightly beat the butter into a block, about 12.5 x 10cm (5x 4inch).

- Roll out the dough on a lightly floured board into a rectangle, 15 x 30cm (6 x 12 inches).

- Place the butter in the centre of the pastry, folding each end over to form a parcel shape. Press the sides together, turn over and let it rest for 10 minutes.

- Roll it out again to 60 x 20cm (24 x 12 inch), fold both ends to the centre and folding in half again to form a square. Allow it to rest again, this time for 20 minutes in the refrigerator.

- Repeat this process four times, then leave the dough covered in the refrigerator until required.

—— INGREDIENTS ——

225g/8oz plain flour

225g/8oz unsalted butter

150ml/¼ pint chilled water

2ml/½ teaspoon salt

5ml/1 teaspoon lemon juice

ELIZABETH RAFFALD'S FAMOUS ECCLES CAKE

— INGREDIENTS —

225g/8oz puff pastry

25g/1oz best butter

100g/4oz currants

25g/1oz mixed peel

50g/2oz mixed fruit

50g/2oz Demerara sugar

2ml/$\frac{1}{2}$ teaspoon mixed spice

2ml/$\frac{1}{2}$ teaspoon freshly grated ginger

2ml/$\frac{1}{2}$ teaspoon fresh grated nutmeg

1 egg white (lightly whisked)

50g/2oz caster sugar

— CHEF'S TIP —
For an even lighter pastry leave the pastry in the refrigerator over night.

— METHOD —

- PRE-HEAT the oven to gas 7/220c/425f.

- Melt the butter in a saucepan.

- Add all the ingredients except the egg white and caster sugar.

- Blend them cook for 4 minutes and allow to cool.

- Roll out the puff pastry until it is very thin.

- Using a saucer or a large pastrycutter, cut it into rounds.

- Place a good tablespoon of the mixture onto each round.

- Gather up the edges, turn over and press with a rolling pin into a flat cake, then shape back into a round.

- Place them onto a dampened baking sheet.

- Brush the tops lightly with the egg white and sprinkle with caster sugar.

- Lower the oven heat to gas 6/200f/400c and bake for 18 to 20 minutes in the centre of the oven, until golden brown.

Eccles cakes are ideal with a little butter or English cheeses garnished with grapes, spring onion, radish, baby beetroot or celery for a special afternoon treat.

MALVERN CHERRY & LEMON CAKE

Worcester is famous for Royal Worcester pottery and Malvern for its mineral water and this very light cherry & lemon cake.

— METHOD —

- PRE-SET the oven to gas 5/190c/375f.

- Grease and line a round cake tin.

- Cream the butter and sugar together until it is fluffy.

- Slowly add the eggs, lemon juice and thin slices of rind.

- Toss the cherries into the flour and place to one side.

- Sift the flour into the mixture.

- Add the cherries and slowly add the milk.

- Pour the mixture into the cake tin and bake for 30 minutes, until it is well risen and firm to the touch.

- Turn the cake onto a wire rack and allow it to cool.

- Lightly dust with icing sugar and decorate with candied lemon.

— INGREDIENTS —

1 lemon, zest and juice

275g/10oz glace cherries

225g/8oz soft butter

225g/8oz caster sugar

4 eggs, beaten

350g/12oz self-raising flour

45ml/3 tablespoon fresh milk

icing sugar

candied lemon

CHOCOLATE & BLACK CHERRY CAKE

*T*his cake, believe it or not, is one of the commonest in British cookery, being served in restaurants around Europe as Black Forest Gateau. It was made in England using home-grown black cherries from around 1840. It is simpler to use tinned black cherries for this recipe.

— INGREDIENTS —

1 tablespoon butter

3 large eggs

175g/6oz castor sugar

175g/6oz plain flour

25g/1oz cocoa powder

2 teaspoons baking powder

4 tablespoons hot water

100g/4oz black cherries, tinned, pitted and tossed in flour

600ml/1 pint double cream

4 tablespoons cherry brandy

450g/1lb black cherries, tinned & pitted

100g/4oz milk chocolate, roughly grated

— METHOD —

● PRE-HEAT the oven to gas 5/375f/190c.

● Lightly grease a 23cm/9 inch round cake tin, lined with greaseproof paper.

● Place into a double boiler or a clean bowl over a pan of simmering water, the eggs and sugar, whisking until the mixture is quite pale and thick.

● Remove the pan or bowl from the heat and whisk for a further 3 minutes.

● Into another clean bowl sift the flour, cocoa and baking powder. Gently whisk in the egg mixture and hot water. Add the cherries and blend them into the mixture.

● Spoon the mixture into the baking tin and bake in the centre of the oven for 40 minutes. Allow it to cool for 10 minutes, then carefully turn the cake out, remove the greaseproof paper and let it cool completely on a wire rack.

● When the cake is completely cold, cut it through the centre, making it into two layers. Whip the cream until stiff and peaky. Pour the cherry brandy onto the centre layer and line with cherries, top with cream, then carefully place the top layer onto it.

● Cover the side and the top with cream garnished with cherries. Sprinkle with the milk chocolate and then chill for one hour before serving.

To slice the cake, use a large knife that has been placed into warm water. Every time you slice, repeat by placing the knife into warm water, this will ensure very even and clean slices of cake.

English Parkin

The battle between Lancashire and Yorkshire still continues on the origin of this recipe. Graham and Rosie Wild, who's families have lived in the Doncaster area, are convinced it really did come from that area, like the Yorkshire Treacle Tart and Mint Pasty. We should agree that no matter what area they come from they are still the best of British products.

Method

● Pre-heat the oven to gas 4/150c/300f.

● Into a large bowl lightly mix the flour and baking powder, oatmeal, ginger, salt, sugar, nutmeg and bicarbonate of soda.

● Melt the treacle and butter in a saucepan and add this to the dry ingredients, slowly adding the milk.

● Line a bread baking tin with grease-proof paper and pour in the mixture.

● Bake in the centre of the oven for 45 minutes.

Ingredients

225g/8oz plain flour

10ml/2teaspoon baking powder

pinch of salt

50g/2oz brown sugar

10ml/2 teaspoon ground ginger

pinch of nutmeg

100g/4oz butter

225g/8oz black treacle

225g/8oz oatmeal

75ml/2floz milk

pinch bicarbonate of soda

SCOTLAND'S OWN - BUTTERSCOTCH TART

*T*his recipe really is special. It originated around the year 1666 when a Scots merchant brought his cargo of West Indian sugar to the Clyde, providing Scotland with a unique dessert. This was also a factor in laying the foundations of the great sugar-refining industry at Greenock.

— INGREDIENTS —

175g/6oz short crust pastry
(see recipe on page 135)

50g/2oz sifted plain flour

175g/6oz Demerara sugar

5 tablespoons water

150ml/¼ pint fresh butter milk

50g/2oz butter

1 egg yolk

pinch ground ginger

2 tablespoons double cream

chopped walnuts

— METHOD —

● PRE-HEAT the oven to gas 5/375f/190c.

● Roll out the pastry, line a 20cm/8 inch flan ring with the pastry and bake blind.

● Place the flour and sugar in a saucepan and gently heat, blending them together, then add the water.

● Boil the buttermilk in another saucepan and pour it over the flour and sugar, blending them thoroughly.

● Cut the butter into small pieces and slowly add it to the pan, stirring all the time. Remove the pan from the heat blend to the egg yolk, ginger and cream. Let it settle for 30 seconds and then blend again.

● Pour the butterscotch into the baked pastry case and top with chopped walnuts.

● Allow it to chill in the refrigerator for at least 1 hour.

BAKING BLIND: Line the raw pastry case with a double sheet of greaseproof paper or cooking foil and fill it with dried peas, beans or rice. This prevents the pastry bubbling during the cooking process.
When the pastry is half baked, which takes 15 minutes, the dried peas and the greaseproof paper.can be removed. The pastry case is then returned to the oven for a further 5 minutes.

The dried peas, beans or rice can be used and re-used over and over again.

ENGLISH HAZELNUT LAYER CAKE

We have hazelnuts in abundance and they were being used in China over 5000 years ago. They are commonly known as the filbert. This name comes from the harvest time in Europe, when the St Philibert feast day starts on the 22nd day of August.

You don't have to use hazelnuts for this recipe, try it with chestnuts, walnuts, almonds or a mixture of all of them with some sultanas for a fruit and nut layer cake.

— METHOD —

● PRE-HEAT the oven to gas 4/350f/180c

● Lightly butter two 25cm/10 inch, loose bottom cake tins. Place the hazelnuts onto a tray and roast them in the oven for 10 minutes. Allow them to cool slightly and put them through a food processor until ground down.

● Put the egg yolks and soft brown sugar into a bowl and beat until light and creamy. Mix in the ground hazelnuts.

● In a separate bowl whisk the egg whites until peaky, then fold the egg whites into the hazelnut mixture.

● Divide the mixture in half and place into the two cake tins, baking them in the centre of the oven for 60 minutes.

● Allow the cakes to completely cool and place onto a wire rack.

● Meanwhile whip the cream with tablespoon of brandy until stiff and peaky.

● Use half the cream and hazelnuts to line and sandwich the cakes. Then top the cake with cream, sprinkle with crushed hazelnuts and garnish the edges with the 12 whole hazelnuts.

— INGREDIENTS —

25g/1oz butter

225g/8oz very finely crushed hazelnuts

5 eggs, separated

150g/5oz soft brown sugar

1 tablespoon brandy

250ml/8floz double cream

100g/4oz crushed hazelnuts, roasted

12 whole hazelnuts

SHORTBREAD LAYERED WITH FRESH STRAWBERRIES

— INGREDIENTS —

225g/8oz plain flour

100g/4oz best butter

50g/2oz castor sugar

1 egg, separated

icing sugar

kebab skewer

450g/1lb fresh strawberries, hulled and halved, soaked in your favourite liquor

— BISCUIT METHOD —

● PRE-HEAT the oven to gas 6/400f/200c.

● Into a large bowl, put the flour and softened butter, rubbing gently with your fingertips until the mixture resembles breadcrumbs.

● Add the sugar, blending thoroughly, then add the egg yolk to bind the mixture together.

● Knead the mixture lightly on a floured board until it is rolled flat, to about 0.5cm/$^1/_4$ inch in thickness.

● Prick the surface with a fork, then cut into rounds with a 7.5cm/3 inch fluted cutter.

● Place the rounds onto a greased baking tray, brush lightly with the egg white and sprinkle with caster sugar.

● Bake for 25 minutes, until they are a light golden brown. Transfer to a wire rack.

● Place one biscuit onto the centre of a plate and evenly cover with strawberries, top with another biscuit and repeat the process.

● Coat the third biscuit with icing sugar. Garnish with a fan of strawberries and other berries.

MANX CAKE

J found this recipe in my copy of *Warnes Model Cookery, 1868, by Mary Jewry*. I thought you might like to
try it, it is very similar to rice cake.
I have converted the recipe for the people of the Isle of Man to enjoy.

METHOD

● PRE-HEAT the oven to gas 5/375f/190c.

● Butter a 18cm/7 inch sandwich cake tin.

● Put the eggs in a blender and blend for 5 minutes, or place
them into a bowl, using a hand whisk blend for 10 minutes.

● Sieve the rice flour into the eggs and blend, add the sugar and
lemon rind and give the mixture a good stir.

● Pour the mixture into the buttered cake tin, cover the top with
a piece of greased, greaseproof paper and bake in the centre of
the oven for 40 minutes.

INGREDIENTS

*Half a pound of rice flour;
half a pound of white sugar;
eight eggs; peel of half a lemon.
Well beat eight eggs for half an
hour, and stir them into half a
pound of rice flour,
half a pound of white sugar
pounded,
and peel of the lemon grated.
Mix well together,
and bake it in a buttered tin.*

25g/1oz butter

225g/8oz rice flour

225g/8oz granulated sugar

8 eggs

grated peel of ¹/₂ lemon

*The Promenade, Douglas,
Isle of Man, 1897.*

GRASMERE GINGERBREAD

*T*his recipe has a great deal of happy memories for all my family. Once a year I visit the Lakes especially to pay homage to one of my favourite shops, Sarah Nelson's in Grasmere, which is tucked away near to the churchyard in Grasmere where William Wordsworth is buried. One day I took my son Matthew to visit Wordsworth's grave. Matthew, only being eight years old at the time and not knowing that Mr Wordsworth the very English poet died 200 years ago, asked me in a very polite manner in front of about 20 Americans, "Have you cooked for him dad?" That says a great deal for my cooking, or is it my age?

Sarah Nelson started baking her gingerbread at this shop in 1855, the recipe is now stored in the vaults of a bank, so I have devised a recipe that is very near to what I have been tasting for the past 15 years, in more of a cake form.

— INGREDIENTS —

225g/8oz self-raising flour

100g/4oz soft brown sugar

1 tablespoon ground ginger

pinch salt

100g/4oz butter

1 large tablespoon golden syrup

2 egg yolks, beaten

100g/4oz mixed chopped peel

2 tablespoons dark rum

white of 1 egg, whisked gently

2 tablespoons soft brown sugar

1 teaspoon ginger

— METHOD —

● PRE-HEAT the oven to gas 3/325f/170c.

● Grease an oblong baking tin, about 20cm/8 inch x 10cm/4 inch.

● Into a bowl, put the flour, sugar, ginger and salt. Melt the butter and syrup in a saucepan over a low heat. Take the pan from the heat and whisk in the egg yolks. Pour this mixture onto the flour ingredients, blending them thoroughly. Soak the mixed peel in the rum for 3 minutes.

● Press half the gingerbread mixture into the tin and sprinkle with the rum flavoured peel, then top with the remaining gingerbread mixture.

● Brush the top with egg white, put the sugar and ginger into a plastic bag and shake it together.

● Sprinkle this onto the surface of the gingerbread and bake in the centre of the oven for 30 to 35 minutes.

REAL SCOTS OATCAKES

hese oatcakes go well with the potted cheese recipes. They were served after the battle of Culloden to the Young Pretenders soldiers in 1746, so they should really be called Bonnie Prince Charlie Oatcakes.

—METHOD—

● PRE HEAT the oven to gas 5/375f/190c.

● Put the oatmeal, sugar, baking powder and salt into a bowl and mix them thoroughly. Add the melted butter and water, blending well.

● Lightly knead the dough with your hands dusted with oatmeal, until it forms into a ball.

● Place the mixture onto a surface sprinkled with oatmeal and roll out the oatcake mixture as thinly as you possibly can. Using a pastry cutter, cut them into round and place onto a greased baking sheet.

● Bake in the centre of the oven for 20 minutes. Allow them to cool and serve with butter or with potted cheese.

—INGREDIENTS—

225g/8oz fine oatmeal

25g/1oz soft brown sugar

$^1/_2$ teaspoon baking powder

pinch salt

25g/1oz melted butter

150ml/$^1/_4$ pint of boiling water

oatmeal for kneading

Rothesay Pier, 1897.

SINGING HINNEY'S

A taste of Tyneside. Hinny is a word meaning a corruption of honey. The cake was cooked on a grid-iron and the cooking sound from the griddle refers to the singing. They were sometimes filled with silver threepenny pieces and given to Geordie children at their birthday parties in the nineteenth century.

INGREDIENTS

350g/12 oz self-raising flour

50g/2oz ground rice

pinch salt

50g/2oz castor sugar

2 teaspoons of baking powder

50g/2oz butter

75g/3oz currants

150ml/¼ pint cream

METHOD

● Place the flour, ground rice, salt, sugar and baking powder into a mixing bowl and blend the ingredients together. Add the butter and rub it into the mixture with your fingertips, until it resembles breadcrumbs. Add the currants and cream to make a soft dough.

● Onto a floured surface, roll the dough to around about 5mm/¼ inch thick. Cut the mixture into quarters and bake on a greased griddle (listen to it sing) or frying pan for 4 minutes on either side, until they a brown. Serve with lashings of butter, jam or clotted cream.

Sunderland Docks, c.1900.

BRANDY SNAPS

 randy Snaps filled with creamed cheese and a little port, served with Eccles cakes and garnished with a poached pear make a very unusual dessert.

— METHOD —

- PRE-HEAT the oven to gas 4/350f/180c.

- Lightly grease three 20cm x 8 inch baking sheets and the handles of a few wooden spoons with the 25g of butter.

- Into a clean dry bowl, sift the flour and ginger. Melt the butter in a saucepan, adding the sugar and syrup. Warm, then remove from the heat, add the flour and ginger stir well, then add the lemon rind and juice, stirring well again.

- Put small tablespoons of the mixture onto the baking sheets, remember to space them well, because the mixture will spread, about six tablespoons per sheet.

- Bake for 10 minutes. Remove from the oven and leave to cool for 10 seconds, until the edges of the brandy snaps begin to firm. Lift them carefully one at a time with a palette knife and roll loosely around the handle of the greased wooden spoons. Allow them to cool before removing them from the handles of the spoon.

- Should they begin to go hard before you roll them onto the handles, return to the oven for a further minute to soften.

— INGREDIENTS —

25g/1oz butter

50g/2oz plain flour

1 teaspoon ground ginger

50g/2oz butter

50g/2oz soft dark brown sugar

2 tablespoons golden syrup

2 tablespoons grated lemon rind

1 teaspoon lemon juice

Sponge fingers & Old Fashioned English Trifle

J have created this recipe for my mothers old fashioned trifle which follows this recipe.

— INGREDIENTS —

Sponge Fingers
25g/1oz butter

caster sugar for dusting

100g/4oz plain flour

3 eggs, separated

100g/4oz castor sugar

Trifle
8 individual sponge fingers
(see the above recipe)

4 tablespoon raspberry jam

3 tablespoons cream sherry

2 tablespoons brandy

25g/1oz flaked almonds

grated rind of ½ lemon

1 custard sauce

300ml/½ pint double cream

25g/1oz crushed almonds

glace cherries

— Sponge Fingers Method —

- Pre-heat the oven to gas 3/325f/160c.

- Grease two 25cm x 10inch baking sheets with the butter and dust the trays lightly with caster sugar.

- Sift the flour into a bowl.

- Blend together the egg yolks and sugar in a mixing bowl, lightly fold in half the flour.

- Whisk the egg whites until they become firm, fold this very lightly into the yolk mixture and add the remaining flour.

— English Trifle Method —

- Take the sponge fingers, coat them with the jam and place them into a glass dish. Sprinkle with sherry, brandy, almonds and the lemon rind.

- Make the custard to the recipe and strain it over the sponge fingers. Allow the custard to go quite cold.

- Whip the cream until it is stiff and spread over the cold custard, decorate with the crushed almonds and glace cherries.

MAIDS OF HONOUR

*T*his recipe is reputed to have been invented by a Richmond baker for Henry VIII's hand maidens.

— METHOD —

● PRE-HEAT the oven to gas 7/425f/220c. Butter a 12 cake/patty tin.

● Gently heat the milk in a saucepan, but do not boil. Add the cake crumbs, butter, sugar, ground almonds, egg, rind of lemon and a few drops of almond essence, stirring all the ingredients together. Then let it stand for 10 minutes.

● Meanwhile make the pastry, roll it out and cut out 12 rounds using a fluted pastry cutter, 7cm/3 inch. Place the pastry into the patty tins and generously spread the base of each one with the strawberry jam. Divide the filling mixture equally into each pastry cup.

● Bake in the centre of the oven for 20 minutes until golden brown. Allow them to cool slightly for 5 minutes, before moving from the patty tins.

— INGREDIENTS —

25g/1oz butter

150ml/¼ pint of milk

25g/1oz cake crumbs

50g/2oz butter, cut into small pieces

25g/1oz castor sugar

50g/2oz ground almonds

1 egg, beaten

rind of 1 lemon, grated

almond essence

175g/6oz shortcrust pastry
(see recipe on page 135)

strawberry jam

Richmond from the bridge, London, 1899.

CHOCOLATE, FRUIT & NUT BISCUITS

 love old fashioned food and I make these for visitors to my home.

— INGREDIENTS —

50g/2oz butter

75g/3oz castor sugar

50g/2oz chopped almonds

50g/2oz chopped hazelnuts

25g/1oz plain flour

50g/2oz sultanas

8 glace cherries, coarsely chopped

3 tablespoons single cream

175g/6oz milk chocolate

— METHOD —

● PRE-HEAT the oven gas to 4/350f/180c. Grease 3 baking sheets.

● Place the butter into a saucepan and gently heat, add all the ingredients except the milk chocolate.

● Cook the mixture for 3 minutes, stirring all the time. Place 1 tablespoon of the biscuit mixture onto the baking sheets, leaving room between each biscuit.

● Bake in the centre of the oven for 10 to 12 minutes. With a pallet knife push any excess from the biscuit into a tidy circle and allow them to cool completely.

● Melt the chocolate in a clean bowl set over boiling water. When the biscuits are cold, turn them over onto a wire rack and coat the underside (smooth side) with the milk chocolate. As the chocolate begins to just set, use a fork to make wavy lines across the base of each biscuit.

CORNISH FAIRINGS

ommonly known as gingernut biscuits and sold in the town of Launceston in Cornwall for centuries.

— METHOD —

- PRE-HEAT the oven to gas 6/400f/200c.

- Lightly grease two non-stick baking sheets and place to one side.

- Sift the flour into a bowl and add a generous pinch of salt, baking powder, bicarbonate of soda, ginger and a generous pinch of cinnamon.

- With your fingertips rub in the softened butter, add the soft brown sugar and warm syrup and mix all the ingredients thoroughly to a stiff consistency.

- Roll the fairings into small balls and place them onto the buttered baking sheets about 10cm/4 inchs apart, allowing for the biscuits to spread.

- Place them into the centre of the oven and bake for 8 minutes until crisp and golden brown.

— INGREDIENTS —

25g/1oz butter

100g/4oz fine plain flour

pinch salt

1 teaspoon baking powder

1 teaspoon bicarbonate of soda

1 tablespoon ground ginger

pinch ground cinnamon

50g/2oz butter, softened

50g/2oz soft brown sugar

3 tablespoons golden syrup

The Square, Lanceston, 1935.

NEWBURGH CINNAMON & CHOCOLATE CHIP BISCUITS

J created this biscuit for Newburgh Fair in Lancashire, during my annual barbecue for the local school. Yes they did sell out! Try them yourself and you will see why. . .

— INGREDIENTS —

25g/1oz butter

25g/1oz plain flour

1 teaspoon baking powder

pinch salt

175g/6oz wholemeal flour

25g/1oz medium oatmeal

1 teaspoon ground cinnamon

2 tablespoons chocolate chips

75g/3oz butter

75ml/5tablespoons milk

— METHOD —

● PRE-HEAT the oven to gas 6/400f/200c. Lightly butter two non-stick baking trays.

● Sift the plain flour, baking powder and a generous pinch of salt into a bowl. Add the wholemeal flour, oatmeal, cinnamon and chocolate chips and blend them thoroughly together.

● Rub in the butter with your fingertips to resemble breadcrumbs, then add the milk and mix to a firm dough.

● Roll the mixture on a floured work surface into a flat square until it is 0.5cm/¼ inch in thickness.

● Cut into squares. Place them onto the baking trays and bake in the centre of the oven for 10 to 12 minutes until they are golden brown. Allow them to cool and serve with fresh coffee.

The Green, Newburgh.

Chapter 9

BREADS

*T*here are two very important things to remember when making bread. I was taught by the best maker of bread products in the North of England, Mr Derrick Warburton, whose historic family started Warburtons bakery in 1870, and they are bakers, born and bread!

*T*he first thing is to ensure that the temperature of the liquid you use to make the dough does not exceed 43c/110f, or this will start to kill the fresh yeast. The second is kneading, this action develops the gluten in the flour.

*T*o knead dough, place it on a lightly floured surface, ensuring that nothing else is in your way. Hold the dough firmly in place with one hand and with the other take hold of part of the end, stretching the dough away from you, folding it back into the centre and pushing it down with the ball of your fist. Turn the dough 35 degrees and repeat the process for 8 to 10 minutes.

Cornfield, Coltishall, 1902.

IRISH SODA BREAD

Where else could I start this section but with one of my favourite breads, Irish soda, served warm with lashings of Irish butter and cheese. I once made this recipe with 75g/3oz sultanas and lightly coated the top of the bread with 1 tablespoon of clear honey, sprinkled with sesame seeds.

— INGREDIENTS —

1 tablespoon bacon or beef dripping

350g/12oz wheatmeal flour

350g/12oz plain white flour

1 teaspoon salt

50g/2oz lard, cut into small pieces

3 teaspoons bicarbonate of soda

2 tablespoons cream of tartar

1 tablespoon soft brown sugar

600ml/1 pint buttermilk or half milk, half single cream

— METHOD —

● Lightly grease a baking tray with the bacon dripping.

● PRE-HEAT the oven to gas 8/450f/230c.

● Place the two flours into a bowl with the salt and blend together. With your fingertips, rub in the lard until the mixture resembles fine breadcrumbs.

● Sprinkle in the bicarbonate of soda, cream of tartar and soft brown sugar, mix them all in together and add the buttermilk. Using your hands, blend and knead the dough very thoroughly.

● Shape the dough into a ball and place onto the baking sheet. Carefully press the ball down to form a disc shape, then cut into quarters. Dust with the wheatmeal flour and bake in the oven for 30-35 minutes.

● Allow the bread to cool for at least 15 minutes before serving. Try this bread fried in bacon fat with white pudding and fried eggs at breakfast time.

TRADITIONAL TEA CAKES

METHOD

- Lightly butter two baking sheets and PRE-HEAT the oven to gas 7/425f/220c.

- Sieve the flour into a large mixing bowl with the salt. With your fingertips, work in the lard until it resembles breadcrumbs.

- Dissolve the sugar in the warmed milk, ensuring the milk does not go over 40c(104f), as this will kill the yeast. Add 4 tablespoons of the milk, to the yeast to make a smooth paste, then add this to the rest of the milk and pour the liquid over the flour.

- Mix until the dough stretches, work in the sultanas and currants, and shape the dough into a ball. Place it into a large, greased bowl, cover with greased cling film and leave it in a warm area for 50 minutes.

- Tip the dough onto a lightly floured surface and knead with the heal of your hand for at least 3 minutes. Reshape again into a ball and cover, leaving the dough to rise again for a further 20 minutes.

- Divide the dough into 10 generous pieces and shape each of them into smooth ball. Roll out the balls to 9cm, about 3 to 4 inches, in size, each teacake 2.5cm/1 inch apart on the buttered baking sheets. Cover with greased cling film and leave them to rise in a warm area for a further 45 minutes.

- Remove the cling film and bake in the centre of the oven for 10 to 12 minutes until golden brown.

INGREDIENTS

25g/1oz butter

450g/1lb strong white flour

teaspoon salt

50g/2oz lard

50g/2oz castor sugar

300ml/$\frac{1}{2}$ pint milk, warmed (40c/104f)

25g/1oz fresh yeast

50g/2oz sultanas

50g/2oz currants

CRUSTY WHITE COTTAGE LOAF WITH HONEY & SESAME SEED

*T*his is one of my own favourite recipes because I live in a cottage, so really all the breads that come out of my ovens are cottage loaves.

You can also use this recipe for normal crusty bread by using 2 x 450g/1lb bread tins and dividing the dough into two.

For a fruitier loaf, add 75g/3oz sultanas with 1 teaspoon of cinnamon with the dry ingredients.

— INGREDIENTS —

25g/1oz butter

450g/1lb strong, white flour

1 teaspoon salt

7g/¹/₄ oz lard

7g/¹/₄ oz yeast

450ml/³/₄ pint warm water

1 tablespoon honey

1 tablespoon sesame seeds

— METHOD —

● Lightly butter a baking tray and PRE-HEAT the oven to gas 7/425f/220c.

● Into a mixing bowl, sieve the flour and salt and rub in the lard. Mix the yeast with 1 tablespoon of the warm water and return to the rest of the water, stirring it well. Add this to the flour, ensuring it is fully blended, and knead the dough for 5 minutes *(see Bread page 173)*.

● Shape the dough into a ball, place it into a warm greased bowl, cover with greased cling film and place in a warm area to rise for 2 hours.

● Turn the dough out onto a lightly floured surface and really press it out with the ball of your hand for 3 minutes, shape back into a ball again, cover with greased cling film and return to the warm area for a further 1 hour.

● Cut off just over one-third of the dough and shape both pieces into large and small balls. Moisten the top of the large ball and place the small one on top of it. Place the loaf onto the greased baking sheet. Push the first three fingers of both hands together and down into the top ball until it reaches the larger ball, sealing the two parts together.

● Cover with greased cling film and let it rise for 40 minutes in a warm area.

● Bake in the centre of the oven for 35 minutes, coat the tops of the bread with the honey and sprinkle with sesame seeds then bake for a further 10 minutes.

BARA BRITH

*T*his speckled bread (Bara Brith) is a really nice bread to go with Caerphilly cheese, for a real taste of North Wales. Originally served in farmhouses and cottages during the Harvest festival, Easter and Yule-tide log burning festival.

— METHOD —

- PRE-HEAT the oven to gas 4/350f/180c.

- Lightly grease with the butter a 900g/2 lb loaf tin or two 450g/1lb loaf tins.

- Sieve the flour and salt into a large mixing bowl, add the lard and rub it into the flour. Add the sugar and spice, mixing again, and make a well in the mixture.

- Blend the egg with the warm water and use two tablespoons to make a smooth paste with the yeast, then blend the paste back into the water.

- Pour into the flour, mixing thoroughly and vigorously, then knead until it is like a smooth but elastic dough consistency. Add the currants, sultanas and mixed fruit, kneading them into the dough.

- Roll it into a round but long shape to fit the loaf tin or divide to fit the two tins.

- Place the tin onto a baking sheet and cover with greased cling film and put in a warm place for 2 hours. Remove the cling film and bake in the centre of the oven for 35 to 40 minutes, until golden brown.

- For a better, crisper topping, add 1 tablespoon of apricot jam to coat the top of the bread and then sprinkle with poppy seed at the 30 minute stage of the baking process. Bake for the last ten minutes and serve with fresh salad and cheese.

— INGREDIENTS —

25g/1oz butter

275g/10oz strong, white flour

1 teaspoon salt

25g/1oz lard

25g/1oz soft brown sugar

1 level teaspoon ground mixed spice

1 large egg, beaten

150ml/$\frac{1}{4}$ pint warm water

25g/1oz fresh yeast

225g/8oz currants

100g/4oz sultanas

BATH BUNS

 nown in the seventeenth century as Royal Bath Buns, they contained no fruit at all until the late eighteenth century, when fruit was a little more common.

—INGREDIENTS—

TO FERMENT THE PRE-MIXTURE:
1 large beaten egg

150ml/5floz warm milk

1 tablespoon sugar

20g/³/₄ oz fresh yeast

50g/2oz strong white flour

Dough

450g/1lb strong, white flour

175g/6oz softened butter

1 egg

175g/6oz coarse sugar
(nibbed or crystallised)

100g/4oz sultanas

50g/2oz candied citrus peel,
chopped

finely grated rind of 1 lemon

1 beaten egg to glaze

coffee crystal sugar for topping

—METHOD—

● PRE-HEAT the oven to gas 7/425f/220c.

● Prepare the ferment pre-mix by stirring the beaten egg into the warm milk, add the sugar and use 3 tablespoons of the warm milk to blend the yeast to a smooth paste in a large bowl. Add the remaining milk and whisk in the flour to make a batter, cover the bowl with cling film and place in a warm area for 30 minutes.

● Blend together the flour, butter and egg, add to the fermented pre-mix and knead the mixture for 10 minutes. Cover with cling film and leave for 60 minutes.

● Place the mixture into a bowl and add the sugar, sultanas, peel and grated lemon rind. Blend the bun mixture and leave for 5 minutes.

● With a tablespoon, place small mounds of the bun mixture onto 2 greased baking trays, cover with cling film and leave to rise for a further 25 minutes.

● Brush the buns over lightly with the beaten egg, sprinkle with the sugar and bake in the centre of the oven for 20 minutes, until golden brown.

Allow them to cool slightly and then serve warm with lashings of butter.

SALLY LUNN LOAF

*A*nother Bath recipe, from a pastry cook who owned a shop in Lilliput Alley in 1782. Bath certainly had a wealth of baking experience with Sally Lunn Teacakes and the famous Pieman of Bath in the 1880's. I am sure this is where Simple Simon met the pieman going to the fair, when Simple Simon said to the pieman "Let me taste your ware".
This sweet bread should be eaten when it is slightly warm with thick clotted cream not butter!

— METHOD —

- PRE-HEAT the oven to gas 8/450f/230c.

- For the ferment, mix the flour, sugar and yeast together in a basin, gradually adding the warm milk to make a thin batter. Cover with cling film and leave in a warm area for 25 minutes.

- For the dough, blend the sugar and flour together and add the beaten egg and lemon rind. Add to the ferment mixture and blend thoroughly, then knead for 10 minutes to make a soft dough.

- Knead in the butter and make the dough into a ball shape. Place into a lightly buttered bowl, cover with cling film and place in a warm area to rise for 30 minutes.

- Cut the dough into three pieces, moulding each piece into a ball shape. Place each ball into a lightly buttered cake tin, covering again with cling film and leave to rise in a warm area for a further 30 minutes. Remove the cling film and lightly brush the tops with the beaten egg. Bake in the centre of the oven for 15 minutes.

- Remove the Sally Lunn Loaves from the oven and allow them to cool for 5 minutes. Try this bread with honey or strawberry jam.

— INGREDIENTS —

FERMENT
50g/2oz strong, white flour

1 tablespoon sugar

20g/$^3/_4$ oz fresh yeast

150ml/5floz warm milk

DOUGH
1 tablespoon sugar

275g/10oz strong, white flour

1 egg, beaten

finely grated rind of 1 lemon

50g/2oz softened butter

1 egg, beaten to glaze

LIVERPOOL CHRISTMAS LOAF

*T*his must be served singing the "Crystal Chandelier" in Liverpool. More of a party loaf, it was the substitute for Christmas cake in the 1920's when the ingredients for the festive cake were hard to come by. Liverpudlians have a unique sense of humour, I know I married one! If you ever want to be cheered up, just come and look at some of the most beautiful buildings dating from the eighteenth to nineteenth century you are ever likely to see in the UK. Meet the people who know that life is worth living, and if you have not visited the Albert Dock, you are missing what 8 million visitors enjoy every year.

— INGREDIENTS —

FERMENT

75ml/2floz warm milk

15g/¹/₂ oz fresh yeast

1 tablespoon sugar

50g/2oz strong, white flour

1 egg, beaten

DOUGH

100g/4oz lard

100g/4oz soft brown sugar

1 egg, beaten

1 tablespoon black treacle

225g/8oz strong, white flour

1 teaspoon salt

1 teaspoon baking powder

1 teaspoon freshly grated nutmeg

1 tablespoon ground mixed spice

225g/8oz sultanas

100g/4oz currants

grated rind of 1 lemon and 1 orange

— METHOD —

● PRE-HEAT the oven to gas 6/400f/200c.

● For the ferment, mix all the ingredients thoroughly together in a warm bowl, cover with cling film and place in a warm area for 25 minutes.

● To make the dough, cream the lard, sugar and egg together and add the treacle with all the rest of the ingredients. Mix them thoroughly together with the ferment mixture.

● Place the dough into a buttered loaf tin, cover with cling film and place in a warm area for 40 minutes. Remove the cling film, place into the centre of the oven and bake for 50 to 60 minutes.

Serve with lashings of butter and fresh strawberry jam (see recipe on page 219).

SELKIRK BANNOCKS

obbie Douglas introduced the Bannock in the mid nineteenth century from his wee shop in Selkirk Market. Traditionally served during the bride's breakfast on the 1st day of Summer and on May Day.

— METHOD —

- PRE-HEAT the oven to gas 6/200c/400f.

- Sieve the flour and salt into a large mixing bowl, roughly rub in the butter and add the sugar to the milk. Use three tablespoons of the milk to blend with the yeast in a large bowl, then slowly add the rest of the milk to the yeast.

- Add the yeast mixture to the flour and butter, mix thoroughly to form a dough and knead for 10 minutes.

- Shape the dough mixture into a ball shape, cover with cling film and place in a warm area to rise for 25 minutes.

- Knead in the sultanas and leave to stand for 20 minutes.

- Divide the dough into two equal pieces and mould each piece into a ball shape. Place onto two baking sheets, cover again with cling film and place into a warm area for 40 minutes. Remove the cling film, flatten the dough to resemble a flat cake and brush lightly with the beaten egg.

- Bake in the centre of the oven for 20 minutes.

— INGREDIENTS —

450g/1lb strong, white flour

1 teaspoon salt

75g/3oz butter

75g/3oz sugar

300ml/10floz warm milk

25g/1oz fresh yeast

450g/1lb sultanas

1 egg, beaten

BREAKFAST LOAFS

hese small Breakfast loaves were commonly known as a MANCHANT, this being a loaf of bread shaped by hand and not baked in a tin. The term is still used today, by bakers in Penzance.

Manchetts for the Queen's Maides
From Ordinances made at Eltham in the seventeenth year of King Henry VIII's realm.
'In the morning one chet lofe, one manchet, one gallon of ale; for afterwards one manchett, one gallon of ale; for after supper one chet lofe, one manchet, two gallon's of ale, dim 'pitcher of wine.'
Only Dukes and Duchesses', Masters of the Household, Clerks of the kitchen and Maids of Honour were served with Manchets in 1526.

Lady Arundel's Manchet, 1676
'Take a bushel of fine wheat flour, twenty egges, and three pounds fresh butter, salt and balm, as to the ordinary manchet, temper it with new milk pretty hot; then let it lie the space of half an hour to rise so you may work it up into bread, and bake it and let not your oven be too hot '.
I have produced this recipe using, as far as is possible, the original ingredients and method.

— INGREDIENTS —

900g/2lb fine wheat flour

1 teaspoon salt

50g/2oz butter

25g/1oz fresh yeast

1tablespoon sugar

1 egg, beaten

600ml/1 pint warm milk

— METHOD —

● PRE-HEAT the oven to gas 6/400f/200c.

● Mix the flour and salt in a large bowl and rub in the butter. Cream the yeast with the sugar and three tablespoons of warm milk. Add the yeast to the rest of the milk with the beaten egg.

● Make a well in the flour and pour in the yeast mixture, blending thoroughly into a dough. Knead the dough for 10 minutes.

● Shape the dough into individual, small, flat round cakes, 2.5cm (1 inch) thick x 7cm (3 inches) rounds. Press them with a palette knife to form diamond shapes, about 2.5cm (1 inch) in length.

● Place them onto a buttered baking sheet, cover with cling film and place in a warm area for 40 minutes. Remove the cling film and bake in the centre of the oven for 20 minutes.

BLACK PUDDING BREAD

I devised this for a Taste of Lancashire in the 1980's and I still think it is one of the tastiest breads I have ever created.

You can also use this recipe for normal crusty bread, by using 2 x 450g/1lb bread tins and dividing the dough into two.

For a fruitier loaf, add 75g/3oz sultanas with 1 teaspoon of cinnamon with the dry ingredients.

— METHOD —

- Lightly butter a baking tray and PRE-HEAT the oven to gas 7/425f/220c.

- Into a mixing bowl, sieve the flour and salt and rub in the lard. Mix the yeast with 1 tablespoon of the warm water and return to the rest of the water, stirring it well. Add this to the flour, ensuring it is fully blended, then knead the dough for 5 minutes.

- Shape the dough into a ball, place it into a warm, greased bowl, cover with greased cling film and leave in a warm area to rise for 2 hours.

- Turn the dough out onto a lightly floured surface and really press it out with the ball of your hand for 3 minutes. Add the crumbs of black pudding to the mixture and shape back into a ball again, cover with greased cling film and return to the warm area for a further 1 hour.

- Cut off just over one-third of the dough and shape both pieces into large and small balls. Moisten the top of the large ball, place the small one on the top of it and place the loaf onto the greased baking sheet. Push the first three fingers of both hands together and press down into the top ball until it reaches the larger ball, sealing the two parts together. Cover with greased cling film and let it rise for 40 minutes in a warm area.

- Bake in the centre of the oven for 35 minutes, coat the tops of the bread with the honey, sprinkle with sesame seeds and bake for a further 10 minutes.

Serve this bread warm with lashings of Irish Butter. . .Enjoy.

— INGREDIENTS —

25g/1oz butter

450g/1lb strong, white flour

1 teaspoon salt

7g/$^1/_4$ oz lard

7g/$^1/_4$ oz yeast

450 ml/$^3/_4$ pint warm water

100g/4oz Irish lean black pudding, crumbled

1 tablespoon honey

1 tablespoon sesame seeds

GRANDMOTHERS BROWN BREAD LANCASHIRE LOAF

*W*hat better way to close this chapter than with this traditional Lancashire loaf?

— INGREDIENTS —

450g/1lb wholemeal or Hovis flour

1 teaspoon salt

7g/¼ oz softened, lard

1 teaspoon soft brown sugar

300ml/10floz warm milk

15g/½ oz fresh yeast

1 tablespoon warm honey

wholemeal flour & poppy seed for sprinkling

— METHOD —

● PRE-HEAT the oven to gas 8/230c/450f.

● Place the wholemeal flour and salt into a bowl and gently rub in the lard, making a well in the centre.

● Add the sugar to the warm milk and whisk until dissolved. Use two tablespoons to blend the yeast into a paste, add the rest of the milk to the yeast and pour into the well.

● Blend the mixture thoroughly, then knead the dough for 10 minutes.

● Shape the dough into a ball and place into a buttered bowl, cover with cling film and place into a warm area to rise for 60 minutes.

● Place the dough onto a wholemeal floured working surface, working out the air, knead for 2 minutes.

● Place the dough into a greased bread tin, cover with cling film and place in a warm area for 30 minutes. Remove the cling film, place into the centre of the oven and bake for 30 minutes.

● Brush the top lightly with honey, sprinkle with the wholemeal flour and poppy seed and return to the oven for a further 10 minutes.

Chapter 10
PUDDINGS & DESSERTS

Forget the diet and forget everything about keeping slim if you are to look at this section. The pudding is one of those recipes that, should you try to skimp on it, with any substitutes, it would be completely ruined.

I am starting this collection with a few traditional favourite savouries that could be forgotten if I did not put pen to paper. They include Beef Steak & Ale Pudding, Somerset Breakfast Pudding, Vegetable Roly Poly and my favourite collection of Yorkshire pudding recipes from my *Heartbeat Country Cookbook*. Tickle those tastebuds with Rosa's Quail Pudding, the original Duchess of Duke Street recipe, then try my Ginger Pudding, Rice, Roly Poly, Semolina, Steamed Treacle, Snowdon Pudding and famous Victorian desserts from around Great Britain.

For all the basic pastry recipes for this section please look under Chapter 8 PIES.

Off the Spoon. . .

BEEF STEAK & ALE PUDDING

— INGREDIENTS —

450g/1lb Suet Pastry
(see recipe on page 125)

flour

1 teaspoon butter

450g/1lb rump of beef,
trimmed weight, cut into cubes

225g/8oz ox kidney, trimmed
weight, diced

1 large onion, peeled and
finely chopped

1 tablespoon plain flour

salt

freshly milled black pepper

1 tablespoon Worcestershire
sauce

1 tablespoon mushroom
ketchup

5 tablespoon stout (Guinness)

300ml/10floz beef stock

— METHOD —

● Roll out the pastry on a floured board, cutting off one third and placing to one side to top the pudding.

● Grease with the teaspoon of butter a 1.8 litre (3 pint) pudding basin and line it with two thirds of the suet pastry. Cover the basin completely, the dough over lapping the edge of the basin.

● Place the beef, kidney and onion into a bowl and sprinkle with flour, seasoning with the salt and freshly milled black pepper. Place the rest of the ingredients into the bowl and blend thoroughly.

● Place the meat filling mixture into the pastry lined pudding basin. Moisten the edge of the pastry with a little milk and place the remaining pastry onto the top of the pudding, pressing and sealing the circular edge together. Trim off any excess pastry.

● Cover the basin with generously greased, grease-proof paper and tie it tightly with string.

● Place the pudding in a large pan with enough boiling water to cover two thirds of the basin. Bring to the boil for 15 minutes, then reduce the heat and steam gently for 4 hours. Remove the greaseproof paper. Place a large serving plate on the top of the pudding and holding the pudding and plate, reverse the pudding onto the plate and serve.

Some of the following recipes are taken from my HEARTBEAT COUNTRY COOKBOOK published by Cassell. I could not resist giving you a generous serving of my Yorkshire pudding recipes, which are based around the characters and places seen in the Heartbeat Yorkshire television series.

Yorkshire Pudding with Minced Turkey & Onion

I do believe this recipe started it's life as lamb, then moved to rabbit, then beef, so you really can please yourself. I'm using turkey breast.

Method

● Pre-heat the oven to gas 7/220c/425f.

● Heat the dripping in a large frying pan, add the minced turkey and chopped onion, and cook for 12 minutes.

● Place a large baking tray and the fat from the minced turkey into the oven for 3 minutes, until it is very hot. The fat should be smoking.

● Pour over the batter and sprinkle with the minced turkey and onion.

● Bake for 30 minutes and serve with a rich gravy.

INGREDIENTS

25g/1oz dripping

225g/8oz minced turkey breast

1 onion, finely chopped

seasoning

Yorkshire pudding batter
(recipe on page 38)

Briggate, Leeds.

CORNED BEEF & BEETROOT PUDDING

orned beef and beetroot go together like peaches and cream, so it will come as no surprise to you to see this recipe.

— INGREDIENTS —

Serves 4

350g/12oz corned beef, cut into small cubes

1 small onion, finely chopped

Yorkshire pudding batter

100g/4oz Red Velvet beetroot, diced

— METHOD —

- PRE-HEAT the oven to gas 7/220c/425f.

- Fry the corned beef and onion in a little dripping for 3 minutes.

- Place a large baking tray and the fat from the corned beef into the oven for 3 minutes, until it is very hot. The fat should be smoking.

- Pour over the batter and sprinkle with the corned beef, onion and beetroot.

- Bake in the centre of the oven for 30 minutes and serve with a tomato sauce.

Right - Market Day, High Street, Skipton, 1893. Far right - Quebec Street, Keighley, c.1890.

TRADITIONAL YORKSHIRE TOAD

The word toad is popular all over England for a quick and simple lunch or supper. If you don't like beef, try it with your favourite cut of meat, poultry or game, ensuring that it is at least half cooked before you cook for the final 20 minutes.

— METHOD —

- PRE-HEAT the oven to gas 8/230c/450f.

- Heat the dripping in a baking tin until it is just smoking.

- Pour in a quarter of the batter and bake for 10 minutes until it is just set.

- While the batter is baking, season and lightly fry the meat until the batter is set. Add the meat to the baking tin, pour in the remainder of the batter, return to the oven and bake for 20 minutes

- Lower the heat (without opening the oven) to gas 6/200c/400f for 15 minutes.

Serve with a red wine sauce or onion gravy.

— INGREDIENTS —

Serves 4

25g/1oz dripping

350g/12oz chuck steak, fat and gristle removed and cubed

salt

freshly milled black pepper

Yorkshire pudding batter
(recipe on page 38)

Kirkgate, Otley, Yorkshire.

ROSA'S QUAIL PUDDING

*T*aken from my book 200 CLASSIC SAUCES, published by Cassell.

"Rosa Lewis' life story was the inspiration for the classic television series *The Duchess of Duke Street*. Much of the script was based on her time as chef/proprietor of my favourite London hotel, the Cavendish in Jermyn Street, (which is on the corner of Duke Street). She was famous for her game sauces and quail pudding, created for her long-time friend Edward VII. Rosa also made her quail pudding for White's, one of London's oldest gentlemen's clubs, and she was advised by Auguste Escoffier, one of her regular clients:

If you don't want to spend the time steaming the pudding, serve the quail meat sliced with vegetables and the sauce in a sauce boat.
If you don't like quail meat, you can try this recipe with breast meat from your favourite game or chicken breast".

For my favourite General Manager, Dee Ludlow at The Cavendish:

— INGREDIENTS —

750g/2oz butter

pinch fine herbs

12 quail breasts, skin removed

75g/3oz button mushrooms

50g/2oz shallots, sliced

150ml/5floz fresh orange juice

1 sprig fresh thyme

2 tablespoons brandy

salt and freshly milled black pepper

150ml/5floz game sauce
(Rowan Yorkshire Jelly page 224)

225g/8oz suet pastry
(see recipe on page 125)

— METHOD —

● Melt the butter in a large frying pan, add the herbs, quail breasts, button mushrooms and shallots and pan-fry them for 6 minutes. Remove the breasts from the pan.

● Add the orange juice, thyme, brandy and seasoning to the pan and simmer for at least 20 minutes, until the liquid is reduced by half.

● Add the game sauce, simmer and reduce by half again. Place the quail meat and game sauce into a 20cm/8 inch pudding basin, which has been buttered and lined with suet pastry.

● Cover the top of the basin with suet pastry and seal, gently brush the top with melted butter and cover with several layers of cooking foil. Steam the pudding in a covered saucepan for 2 hours, topping up the pan with extra water as necessary.

Serve with fresh vegetables

TURKEY & CHESTNUT PUDDING

*I*t was far easier to steam puddings than to bake pies in Edwardian times. With the lack of fuel, a pot could be placed onto the fire and steaming puddings became very popular. This pudding was first called swan pudding, then it became goose and chestnut to taste like swan pudding. The thought of cooking a beautiful bird like a swan appals me today. Thanks to Her Majesty the Queen, the swan can no longer become part of the festivities. When I tried this recipe with goose I found it was not the right meat so I replaced it with turkey, which was used on a regular basis in Norfolk and throughout Victorian England. This recipe being a particular favourite of the Prince Regent.

— METHOD —

● REPEAT PROCESS as on page 186 for Steak 'n' Kidney Pudding in this chapter. . . only steam for 3 hours.

You can also, should you wish, substitute the turkey for game with chestnut or chicken and ham.

The Village, Coltishall, 1902.

— INGREDIENTS —

500g/1lb suet pastry

500g/1lb turkey meat, diced

225g/8oz streaky bacon, rindless, diced

1 onion, peeled, finely chopped

1 tablespoon plain flour

2 tablespoons chopped parsley

pinch nutmeg

225g/8oz chestnuts, shells removed, weight

salt

freshly milled black pepper

3 tablespoons brandy

1 teaspoon clear honey, warmed

300ml/10floz chicken stock

DURHAM VEGETABLE ROLY-POLY

The following three recipes are my *Digging for Victory Recipes* I created for a television show in the North of England, showing the public what a family of four lived on during the war. I have, of course, put them into a more modern and tastier recipe than when they were originally served. There was no butter, cream, milk or eggs; it was margarine, dried milk and dried eggs.
We don't know how lucky we are today. . . . .

— INGREDIENTS —

2 large carrots, peeled and grated

1 turnip, peeled and grated

1 onion, peeled and chopped

4 large potatoes, peeled and grated

4 tablespoons peas

1 teaspoon mixed herbs

salt

freshly milled black pepper

1 tablespoon Worcestershire sauce

2 tablespoons sweet chutney

PASTRY
75g/3oz shredded suet

275g/10oz plain flour

50g/2oz grated raw potato

1 teaspoon baking powder

pinch of salt

— METHOD —

● Make the suet pastry by rubbing the shredded suet into the flour and adding the raw potato, baking powder and pinch of salt. Mix with a little cold water, making the pastry stiff.

● Roll out the pastry on a floured board to a rectangle shape.

● Put all the vegetables into a saucepan with enough boiling water to just cover them and no more. Cook for 15 minutes, then strain until quite dry, keeping the liquid for the gravy.

● Spread the mixed vegetables onto the suet pastry, seasoning with Worcestershire sauce and spreading over the chutney. Season and then roll it up like a Swiss roll, Tie it in greaseproof paper and steam for 2 hours.

● Serve with a gravy made from the vegetable water, thickened with cornflour and gravy browning.

Old Elvet, Durham, 1914.

SOMERSET BREAKFAST PUDDING

here was a shortage of bacon during the war, although American and Canadian bacon could be found for the right price. But yet again I have converted this humble recipe, so that you can enjoy it.

— INGREDIENTS —

100g/4oz shredded suet

350g/12oz plain flour

1 teaspoon baking powder

75g/3oz grated raw potato

salt

1 egg

275g/10oz middle cut bacon, rindless, grilled until crisp and chopped

175g/6oz button mushrooms, sliced

3 tablespoons warm honey

2 eggs, beaten with a little milk

salt

freshly milled black pepper

— METHOD —

● Place the suet, flour and baking powder into a large bowl and mix the ingredients together. Add the raw potato, salt and egg with a little water to make the suet pastry.

● Roll out the suet pastry on a floured board. Grease a medium size pudding basin with a little butter and line the basin with a quarter of the pastry.

● Place the chopped bacon, mushrooms, honey and egg into another bowl and blend the mixture together, seasoning well with salt and pepper.

● Place a third of the mixture into the bottom of the pudding basin and top with another layer of suet. Repeat this process two more times, finishing with the final layer of suet.

● Cover that with a layer of well greased, grease-proof paper, tie it tight with string and steam for three hours.

WARTIME SCOTCH CHEESE PUDDING

 have modernised this. Just slightly!

—METHOD—

- PRE-HEAT the oven to gas 4/350f/180c.

- Place the butter and milk in a saucepan and just warm it over a low heat.

- Mix the breadcrumbs and cheese together in a clean bowl and season with salt and freshly milled black pepper.

- Pour the milk over the cheese mixture, adding the eggs, cream and mustard. Blend the mixture thoroughly, place in a buttered pie dish and bake for 40 to 45 minutes.

—INGREDIENTS—

100g/4oz butter

450ml/³/₄ pint of fresh milk

350g/12oz breadcrumbs

225g/8oz Scottish Cheddar, grated

2 eggs, beaten with 2 tablespoons double cream

1 teaspoon English mustard

salt

freshly milled black pepper

Propaganda poster World War Two.

CUMBERLAND PUDDING

— INGREDIENTS —

450g/1lb cooking apples,
peeled, cored and roughly
chopped

100g/4oz shredded suet

200g/7oz plain flour

2 teaspoon baking powder

150g/5oz currants

75g/3oz soft brown sugar

freshly grated nutmeg

2 eggs, beaten

5 tablespoons milk

25g/1oz butter

soft light brown sugar

— METHOD —

● Place the apples, suet, flour, baking powder, currants, sugar and freshly grated nutmeg into a large bowl and mix the ingredients well.

● Add the beaten eggs with the milk and blend thoroughly. Leave the mixture to stand for 1 hour.

● Grease a 750ml pudding basin with the butter. Give the pudding mixture a final stir and pour it into the greased pudding basin. Cover the pudding basin with a piece of buttered greaseproof paper or cooking foil and secure it with string.

● Place the basin in a large saucepan and fill it with boiling water to just a third from the top of the basin. Cover the pan tightly and steam gently for 2 hours, topping up with water should it be required.

Leave the pudding to stand for 10 minutes then turn it out onto a warm serving plate and sprinkle with the soft brown sugar.

Windermere above Waterhead, 1912.

GINGER PUDDING

—METHOD—

● Sift the flour, ground ginger, salt and soda into a mixing bowl. Add the suet and sugar and mix lightly with your fingers.

● In a separate bowl, pour the treacle, freshly grated ginger, eggs and milk and whisk it all together. Then pour the liquid onto the dry ingredients, blending all the ingredients together to give a soft mixture.

● Grease a 1 litre pudding basin with some butter and pour in the mixture. Cover the basin with grease-proof paper or cooking foil and secure with string.

A Ginger Cake Seller, 1884.

● Place the pudding into a large saucepan with boiling water, the water should come to a third from the top of the basin. Cover the pan tightly with a lid and steam the pudding over a medium heat for 2 hours, topping up with water, should it be needed.

Leave the pudding to stand for 10 minutes, then place onto a warm serving plate and serve with a Ginger Sauce.

— INGREDIENTS —

200g/7oz plain flour

1 teaspoon ground ginger

pinch of salt

1 teaspoon bicarbonate of soda

100g/4oz shredded suet

75g/3oz castor sugar

1 tablespoon black treacle

1 teaspoon freshly grated ginger

1 egg, beaten with 3 tablespoons milk

25g/1oz butter

ICKY'S STICKY TOFFEE PUDDING

I would like to think that everyone in Great Britain has visited The Lakes at some time in their life. Of all my years in the industry, with chefs young and old, the name Francis Coulson reflects traditional British food at its best. No better person than Francis himself could make this classical dish, for which Sharrow Bay Country House Hotel is so greatly renowned.

— INGREDIENTS —

FOR THE SPONGE

50g/2oz best butter

180g/6oz granulated sugar

2 fresh eggs

180g/6oz dates (chopped)

275ml/^{1}/$_2$ pint water

5ml/1 teaspoon bicarbonate of soda

180g/6oz self-raising flour

vanilla essence

FOR THE SAUCE

580ml/1 pint double cream

75g/3oz Demerara sugar

15ml/1 tablespoon black treacle

—CHEF'S TIP—

It is really better to boil the dates with the bicarbonate of soda a few hours before starting the recipe.

—METHOD—

- PRE-SET the oven to gas 4/350f/180c.

- Cream the butter and sugar together in a large, clean bowl.

- Boil the dates in 275ml/^{1}/$_2$ pint water with the bicarbonate of soda.

- Beat the eggs into the butter, gradually adding the flour, dates and water from the dates with a few drops of vanilla essence.

- Pour the mixture into a greased baking tin.

- Finally, bake in the oven for 40 to 45 minutes.

—SAUCE METHOD—

- Put all the sauce ingredients into a large sauce pan and bring to the boil, then simmer for 10 minutes until reduced.

- Pour over the sponge and place it under a grill, until it bubbles.

Serve with a little double cream or fromage frais.

SNOWDON PUDDING

— METHOD —

- Grease a 1 litre pudding basin with the butter and decorate the base with half of the glace cherries and some raisins.

- Into a bowl, add the rest of the cherries, raisins, breadcrumbs, suet, rice, sugar, lemon rind, salt and marmalade, blending all the ingredients together.

- Add the beaten egg and milk and mix the ingredients to form a soft paste mixture. Then spoon it into the pudding basin, cover with grease-proof paper or cooking foil and secure it with string.

- Place the basin into a half filled pan of boiling water, cover with a tight fitting lid and steam for just over 2 hours.

- Let it stand for 10 minutes, then turn it out onto a warm serving plate with a Whisky Sauce *(Traditional Whiskey Sauce page 231)*.

— INGREDIENTS —

25g/1oz butter

50g/2oz glace cherries, halved

100g/4oz raisins

100g/4oz white breadcrumbs

100g/4oz shredded suet

25g/1oz ground rice

100g/4oz castor sugar

grated rind of 1 lemon

pinch salt

2 tablespoons marmalade

2 eggs, beaten with
5 tablespoons milk

Snowdon Mountain Railway, 1896.

TREACLE PUDDING

his always reminds me of school dinners, green gym knickers and soggy cabbage!

— INGREDIENTS —

25g/1oz butter

75g/3oz breadcrumbs

grated rind of 1 lemon

200g/7oz treacle or golden syrup

SUET CRUST PASTRY
300g/11oz plain flour

pinch salt

2 teaspoons baking powder

150g/3oz shredded suet

flour

— METHOD —

• Lightly grease a 1 litre pudding basin and prepare a large saucepan, half filled with boiling water and with a tight fitting lid.

• To make the pastry, sift the flour, salt and baking power into a clean dry mixing bowl. Add the suet and about 250ml/8floz cold water to make a dough, dividing the dough into two onto a floured surface.

• Roll out the first portion to make a round 1cm/^{1}/$_2$ inch larger than the top of the pudding basin.

• Place the remaining pastry into the basin and press it to mould all around the inside of the basin, easing it evenly up the sides to the top.

• Use the remaining portion of pastry to make a lid to fit the top of the basin and the rest to make two rounds to fit the basin at two levels.

• Place a layer of treacle onto the base of the pudding, sprinkle with some of the breadcrumbs and lemon rind, cover with a pastry round and repeat the process until all the ingredients are used, finishing with the pastry lid.

• Cover the pudding with grease-proof paper or cooking foil and secure with string. Place the pudding into the saucepan with the boiling water, secure the lid and steam for two and half hours.

• Leave for 10 minutes to stand, then very carefully turn the pudding out onto a warm serving plate and serve with double cream or vanilla ice cream.

NEWCASTLE CHOCOLATE PUDDING

— METHOD —

● Butter the inside of a 1 litre pudding basin.

● Place the grated chocolate and milk into a saucepan and heat slowly to dissolve and blend the chocolate with the milk.

● Place the butter and sugar into a bowl and cream them together. Beat in the egg yolks. Add the melted chocolate mixture and blend in the breadcrumbs and the baking powder.

● In a separate bowl, whisk the egg whites until they are stiff and carefully fold them into the pudding mixture.

● Spoon the mixture in to the greased pudding basin and cover with grease-proof paper or cooking foil. Secure it with string and place the basin into a pan, half filled with boiling water. Place on a tight fitting lid and gently simmer for 80 minutes.

● Let the pudding stand for 10 minutes, then carefully turn the chocolate pudding onto a warm serving plate and serve with a rich chocolate sauce.

— INGREDIENTS —

25g/1oz butter

50g/2oz plain chocolate, grated

125ml/4floz fresh milk

40g/2oz butter

40g/2oz caster sugar

2 eggs, separated

100g/4oz white breadcrumbs

$^{1}/_{4}$ teaspoon baking powder

Quayside, Newcastle-upon-Tyne, 1928.

SEMOLINA PUDDING

ry adding here two tablespoons of your favourite liquor or spirit for an additional flavour.

— INGREDIENTS —

1 litre/1³/₄ pints of fresh milk

¹/₂ a freshly grated nutmeg

75g/3oz semolina

75g/3oz castor sugar

25g/1oz butter

— METHOD —

● Warm the milk in a large saucepan and add the freshly grated nutmeg. Let the milk (infuse) stand for 10 minutes.

● Warm the milk again and sprinkle with the semolina, whisking it quickly to prevent it going lumpy. Bring the pan to simmering point, stirring all the time for 15 minutes.

● Add the sugar and whisk.

● Butter a 1 litre pudding basin and pour in the semolina. Add the left over butter to the semolina and bake in the centre of the oven for 30 minutes, until golden brown. Gas 3/325f/160c.

Durley Village, 1907.

RICE PUDDING

When my mother used to make rice pudding for our family, the first to the table got the skin!

— METHOD —

- Butter a 1.75 litre/3 pint pudding or pie dish.

- PRE-HEAT the oven to gas 2/300f/150c.

- Wash the rice in cold water for 5 minutes, drain and put it into the dish with the milk. Let the dish stand for 45 minutes.

- Add the sugar and stir. Add the flakes of butter and freshly grated nutmeg.

- Bake in the centre of the oven for 2-3 hours until the pudding is thick and creamy, with a skin and brown on top.

— INGREDIENTS —

25g/1oz butter

100g/4oz pudding rice

1 litre/1 ¾ pints fresh milk

75g/3oz castor sugar

25g/1oz butter, flaked

¼ of freshly grated nutmeg

Ye Olde Tea House..

BREAD & BUTTER PUDDING

nother way of adding extra flavour to this recipe is to butter the bread then spread on your favourite jam.

— INGREDIENTS —

50g/2oz butter

12 slices bread, buttered

175g/6oz sultanas

1 freshly ground nutmeg

400ml/14floz milk

2 large eggs

25g/1oz brown sugar

25g/1oz granulated sugar

— METHOD —

- Butter a 2 litre pie dish, cut the bread into triangles and arrange in alternate layers, butter side up. Sprinkle with sultanas and then grated nutmeg and repeat the process.

- Heat the milk in a saucepan, but do not let it boil.

- Place the two eggs into a bowl with the brown sugar, beat with a whisk and slowly add the hot milk.

- Pour the egg mixture over the bread, sprinkle with the granulated sugar and grated nutmeg and leave it to stand for 45 minutes.

- PRE-HEAT the oven to gas 4/350f/180c.

- Bake in the centre of the oven for 40 minutes, until the custard in the bread and butter pudding is set.

CABINET PUDDING

— METHOD —

● Lightly butter a 1 litre/1¾ pint pudding basin and decorate the base and sides by firmly pressing on 25g/1oz raisins.

● Put the pieces of bread into a bowl and and gently heat the milk, (DO NOT BOIL).

● Place the eggs and sugar into another bowl mix them together, and add the milk, remaining raisins and lemon rind.

● Pour the mixture over the bread and leave it to stand for 15 minutes. Pour the bread mixture into the pudding basin, cover with grease-proof paper or buttered cooking foil and secure with string.

● Place it into a steamer or into a saucepan, half filled with water. Cover with a lid and steam gently for 80 minutes, topping up with water when necessary.

● Remove the pudding and allow it to stand for 5 minutes, then turn out and serve with warmed Strawberry Jam *(recipe on page 219)* or a custard sauce.

— INGREDIENTS —

25g/1oz butter

100g/4oz raisins

4 slices white bread, crust removed and diced 5mm/¼ inch pieces

400ml/14floz milk

3 large eggs

25g/1oz castor sugar

1 teaspoon freshly grated lemon rind

Children Selling.

NEWMARKET PUDDING

— INGREDIENTS —

25g/1oz butter

5 tablespoon redcurrant jelly

6 individual trifle sponges

50g/2oz cut, mixed peel

50g/2oz raisins

25g/1oz currants

400ml/7floz hot milk

3 eggs, beaten with a few drops
of vanilla essence

— METHOD —

● Grease a 13cm/5 inch round cake tin with the butter. Warm the redcurrant jelly and pour it into the bottom of the cake tin.

● Cut the trifle sponge vertically into 1cm/$^1/_2$ inch slices.

● Then alternate the trifle sponge and fruits into the cake tin.

● Whisk the eggs and hot milk (not boiling) together and pour over the sponge and fruit. Let it stand for 30 minutes.

● Cover the top of the cake tin with greaseproof paper or buttered cooking foil and secure with string. Place the cake tin into a saucepan, add enough boiling water to come halfway up the sides of the tin, cover the pan tightly with a lid and steam over a gentle heat for 1 hour.

● Remove the pudding and let it stand for 5 minutes. Turn onto a warm plate and serve with some clotted cream.

High Street, Newmarket, 1929.

CUSTARD TART

his recipe comes from my revised Mrs Beeton, 1861 edition.

METHOD

- PRE-HEAT the oven to gas 6/400f/200c.

- Butter a 18cm/7 inch flan ring on a non-stick baking sheet and line the ring with cooking foil.

- Make the pastry, roll it out on a floured surface and line the flan ring with the pastry.

- Place the eggs and sugar into a bowl and blend together. Add the milk, whisk thoroughly and pour onto the pastry.

- Grate the nutmeg over the top of the custard mixture, place in the oven and bake for 8 minutes.

- Lower the heat to gas 2/300f/150c and bake for a further 20 minutes, until the custard is set.

- Let the custard tart stand for 5 minutes, then carefully remove the flan ring and serve.

INGREDIENTS

shortcrust pastry
(see recipe on page 135)

butter

2 large eggs

50g/2oz caster sugar

250ml/8floz warm milk

freshly grated nutmeg

BLUEBERRY PIE

*M*ention blueberries, black berries or bilberries and my boys go mad. Served just warm with home-made vanilla ice cream, they automatically clean their bedrooms!
You can use any of your favourite berries for this pie.

— INGREDIENTS —

shortcrust pastry
(see recipe on page 135)

900g/2lb fresh blueberries

100g/4oz castor sugar

2 tablespoons plain flour

1 teaspoon lemon rind

1 tablespoon butter

1 tablespoon lemon juice

— METHOD —

● PRE-HEAT the oven to gas 6/400f/200c.

● Roll out the pastry on a lightly floured surface and use two thirds to line a buttered pie dish, 25cm/10in. Save the remainder of the pastry to place onto the top of the pie.

● Place the blueberries, sugar, flour, lemon rind and juice into a bowl and mix thoroughly.

● Spoon the mixture into the lined pie case and dot with the butter.

● Dampen the edge of the pie and place on the pastry lid, sealing the edges. Make two cuts in the top of the pie and bake for 35 minutes.

● Remove the pie from the oven and allow it to stand for 10 minutes before serving.

Saltwood Castle, 1902.

BAKEWELL PUDDING

— METHOD —

- PRE-HEAT the oven to gas 6/400f/200c.

- Make up the pastry and roll it out on a lightly floured surface. Place a 18cm/7 inch flan ring onto a nonstick baking sheet.

- Line the flan ring with the pastry. Spread the jam onto the base of the pastry.

- Blend the butter and sugar together in a bowl. Beat in the egg, cake crumbs, almonds and a few drops of vanilla essence, mixing well.

- Pour the bakewell mixture into the lined pastry and bake in the centre of the oven for 30 minutes.

This is really nice served with warm honey.

— INGREDIENTS —

shortcrust pastry
(see recipe on page 135)

3 tablespoons raspberry jam

50g/2oz butter

50g/2oz castor sugar

1 large egg

50g/2oz cake crumbs

50g/2oz ground almonds

vanilla essence

The Square & Church, Bakewell.

NORTHCOTES APPLE CRUMBLE SOUFFLÉ
& LANCASHIRE CHEESE ICE CREAM

rom a great Northern chef, my dear friend Nigel Howarth, a classical Northern recipe from his restaurant Northecote Manor at Langho.

— INGREDIENTS —

CREME PATISERE
290 ml/10floz milk

1/2 vanilla pod

3 egg yolks

40g castor sugar

50g plain flour, sieved

APPLE PUREE
4 Bramley apples, peeled cored and sliced

85g/3oz castor sugar

EGG WHITES
8 egg whites

3 dessert spoons castor sugar

pinch salt and sugar

CRUMBLE TOPPING
16g plain flour

10g soft butter

10g granulated sugar

— CREME PATISERE METHOD —

● Boil the milk. Whisk together the egg yolks, sugar and sifted flour, mixing well.

● Slowly add the boiling milk, whisking thoroughly. Pour the mixture into a clean saucepan and cook gently until the sauce thickens, for 2 minutes.

● Remove from the heat and allow the creme patisiere to cool, then cover with cling film.

— APPLE PUREE METHOD —

● Cook the apples with the sugar until soft and blend them to a pulp. Place to one side

— CRUMBLE TOPPING METHOD —

● Rub the flour and butter together, add the sugar, place on a baking tray and bake in the oven at gas 4/180c/350f for 15 minutes.

Northcotes Apple Crumble Soufflé
& Lancashire Cheese Ice Cream

— Cheese Ice Cream Method —

- Bring the cream and milk to the boil. Blend the egg yolks and sugar and add one third of the hot milk mixture to the egg yolks.

- Slowly blend in the remaining milk and pass this through a fine sieve.

- Allow the mixture to cool slightly, then whisk in the cheeses thoroughly.

— Apple Baskets Method —

- Slice the apples very thinly into very fine apple rings and place onto a non-stick baking sheet. Sprinkle with castor sugar and bake in the oven for 5 minutes.

- Allow the apples to cool slightly. Place the apple rings around a dariole mould or small teacup overlapping as you go to form a basket. Allow them to set and remove.

— Soufflé Method —

- Using small individual soufflé forms, brush the sides of the soufflé dishes, (6) sprinkle with castor sugar and then pour out again. The soufflé is now lined.

- Reheat the creme patissiere, adding the puree and whisking all the time until it becomes a smooth paste. Pour into a medium size bowl and reserve.

- Take the egg whites, pinch of salt and sugar and beat until soft peaks. Add 3 dessertspoons of castor sugar. With a plastic spatula, carefully fold in to the egg whites, then carefully fill each soufflé to the top, tap the dish onto the table, smoothing off the top.

- With a small, pointed edged knife work around the inside rim of the form and leave a small channel all around. Place onto a baking tray and bake in the oven for 12 minutes.

When ready place the apple basket onto your serving plates, ball up the ice cream and place into the apple basket. Take out each soufflé, sprinkle with crumble mix, dust with icing sugar and serve. Heaven!and worth all the hard work. Thanks Nigel. . . . .

— INGREDIENTS —

LANCASHIRE CHEESE ICE CREAM

200ml double cream

200ml Milk

5 egg yolks

85g castor sugar

140g Philadelphia cheese

85g grated Butlers Lancashire cheese

APPLE BASKETS

2 Coxs apples

castor sugar

TO ASSEMBLE & SERVE THE SOUFFLÉ

3 large tablespoons creme patissiere

4 tablespoons apple puree

LEMON MERINGUE PIE

ne of those recipes my mother used to make every weekend.

— INGREDIENTS —

shortcrust pastry
(see recipe on page 135)

450g/1lb dried peas

300g/11oz granulated sugar

3 tablespoons cornflour

3 tablespoons plain flour

300ml/½ pint boiling water

25g/1oz salted butter

1 teaspoon grated lemon rind

4 tablespoons lemon juice

3 large eggs, separated

50g/2oz castor sugar

— METHOD —

● PRE-HEAT the oven to gas 6/400f/200c.

● Make the pastry and roll it out on a floured surface. Lightly grease a 23cm/9inch pie dish and line with the shortcrust pastry.

● Cover the pastry with grease-proof paper and fill with the dried peas. Bake in the oven for 15 minutes, remove the peas and paper, returning the empty pie to the oven for a further 5 minutes, then allow it to cool.

● Mix the sugar, cornflour and plain flour in a clean bowl, fitted into a saucepan half filled with boiling water, or in the top of a double boiler. Slowly add the boiling water and simmer gently for 20 minutes.

● Take the pan off the heat add the butter, lemon rind and lemon juice and blend.

● Put the egg yolks into a bowl, whisk and add 3 tablespoons of the cooked mixture. Whisk and add to the mixture in the pan, whisk again and cook until the mixture thickens, stirring all the time.

● Place the lemon sauce mixture to one side to cool then pour into the pastry case.

● Whisk the egg whites in a grease free bowl, folding in the sugar. Cover the top of the lemon sauce with the meringue mixture, peaking it outwards with a fork.

● Lower the oven to gas 4/350f/180c and bake for 12 minutes, until the meringue is golden brown.

Allow the pie to cool and serve with double cream.

MANCHESTER PUDDING

*E*verybody knows that Manchester is famous for its football teams, Granada Television and Coronation Street, but did you also know it has a very famous pudding!

— METHOD —

- PRE-HEAT the oven to gas 6/400f/200c.

- Roll out the puff pastry on a floured surface and line a 750ml/1¼ pint pie dish with it.

- Put the milk and lemon rind into a saucepan and heat gently but do not boil. Remove the pan from the heat and leave the milk and lemon to infuse for 15 minutes.

- Place the breadcrumbs into a bowl and strain the lemon flavoured milk over them. Return the mixture to a saucepan and simmer for 3 minutes.

- Blend the eggs and egg yolks into the mixture, with the softened butter and sugar.

- Spread the strawberry jam over the base of the pastry, pour in the breadcrumb mixture and bake for 10 minutes. Lower the heat on the oven to gas 4/350f/180c and bake for 1 hour.

Leave the pudding to cool and serve with custard.

— INGREDIENTS —

puff pastry *(see recipe on page 135)* or buy frozen

250ml/8floz milk

4 strips lemon rind

75g/3oz white breadcrumbs

2 large eggs

2 egg yolks

50g/2oz butter, softened

25g/1oz castor sugar

4 tablespoons strawberry jam

EVES PUDDING

*E*ves pudding is very similar to doing an apple crumble. You can use any fruit like rhubarb, plums, peaches or gooseberries for this recipe, should you wish to do so. I am using apples, which is the original recipe.

— INGREDIENTS —

butter for greasing

900g/2lb cooking apples,
peeled, cored and thinly sliced

grated rind and juice of
1 lemon

75g/3oz Demerara sugar

3 tablespoons dry sherry

75g/3oz butter

75g/3oz castor sugar

1 large egg, beaten

100g/4oz self-raising flour

— METHOD —

● PRE-HEAT the oven to gas 4/350f/180c.

● Lightly butter a 1 litre pie dish, add the sliced apples and sprinkle with lemon juice, Demerara sugar and sherry.

● Cream the butter and sugar in a bowl until fluffy, add the beaten egg and the flour and spread the mixture over the apples. Bake in the centre of the oven for 40 minutes.

Serve with Devon cream.

Northam Village, Devon, 1890.

JAM ROLLY POLY

$\mathcal{T}$he filling possibilities for this recipe are endless, you can use any of your favourite jams and fruits. Try it also with dried fruits soaked in a liquor.

— METHOD —

● PRE-HEAT the oven to gas 5/375f/190c.

● Sift the flour and baking powder into a bowl, add the suet and a little cold water to make a soft dough.

● Roll the dough out on a floured surface, to about 5mm/$^1/_4$ inch in thickness, into a rectangle shape.

● Spread the jam almost to the edge of the pastry then dampen the edges with a little milk or water. Roll up like a swiss roll, sealing the edges at both ends.

● Lightly grease a non-stick baking sheet and place the jam roly poly it. Cover very loosely with greased, grease-proof paper or greased baking foil and bake in the centre of the oven for 50 minutes.

● Carefully remove the roly poly from the oven. Remove the foil and place onto a warm plate and serve with warmed jam or honey.

— INGREDIENTS —

300g/11oz plain flour

1 teaspoon baking powder

150g/5oz shredded suet

flour

300g/11oz raspberry Jam

25g/1oz butter

OXFORD ORANGE TART

his recipe is very similar to a lemon meringue pie and was a favourite of George lll and Queen Charlotte.

— INGREDIENTS —

225g/8oz shortcrust pastry
(see recipe on page 135)

finely grated rind of
3 large oranges

finely grated rind and juice of
1 lemon

400ml/14floz fresh orange juice

150g/5oz castor sugar

3 tablespoons cornflour

5 large eggs, separated

— METHOD —

- PREHEAT the oven to gas 6/400f/200c.

- Line a flan tin *(see Lemon Meringue recipe page 212)* and bake blind.

- Mix together the orange, lemon rinds, orange juice, 100g/4oz sugar and the cornflour in a saucepan. Blend them thoroughly with a whisk and slowly bring to the boil, stirring constantly.

- Remove from the heat and stir in the juice of the lemon and 5 egg yolks. Pour the orange sauce mixture into the baked pastry case.

- Lower the heat on the oven to gas 2/300f/150c.

- In a separate bowl, beat the egg whites and remaining sugar until they become peaky.

- Place the meringue on to the top of the pie filling, covering it completely, using a fork to form little peaks.

- Return the Orange Tart to the oven and bake for 25 to 30 minutes.

Chapter 11

JAMS, PRESERVES, SAUCES & PICKLES

Always choose firm-ripe fruits, never use over-ripe fruit or the jam will not set. The only fruit that should be under-ripe are gooseberries, which are plentiful here in Great Britain.

Today you can buy sugar with pectin in most superstores, this ensures a quicker and guaranteed setting. Silver Spoon, who are based in Peterborough, make this preserving sugar.

If you can, use a large heavy based saucepan or preserving pan when ever you are making jams or preserves.

When potting preserves make sure the jars are clean, dry and warm. Fill the jars to the brim with the Hot, finished jam, preserve or jelly.

Cover with a round of greaseproof paper. Use plastic coated twist tops and seal while the preserves are hot. Label and date each jar and store in a dry, cool and dark area. Most preserves will keep for up to 12 months.

Strawberry Seller, London, 1885.

CHERRY & LOGANBERRY JAM

oganberries are seen throughout Great Britain during the summer months. You can use any berry with cherries for this recipe.

— INGREDIENTS —

1kg/2lb Morello cherries

1kg/2lb loganberries

2kg/4lb sugar with pectin

— METHOD —

● Place the fruits into a large saucepan and simmer gently for 10 minutes, allowing the juices to run.

● Add the sugar and heat gently, stirring all the time until the sugar and pectin has dissolved. Bring to the boil rapidly for 20 minutes. Pour into warm, clean jars and seal. Allow the jam to mature for at least 7 days before use.

Castle Combe, 1907.

STRAWBERRY JAM

When using any of the following jam recipes always use sugar that has pectin in it.
Should you wish to, use your favourite fruit to replace strawberries, using the same method.

— METHOD —

● Hull and wash the strawberries and drain them well and cut them into quarters. Place the strawberries in a large bowl in layers with the sugar and pectin, leaving them for 3 hours.

● Put them into a large saucepan, add the lemon with rind and stir for 2 minutes, until the lemon is blended.

● Bring to the boil rapidly for 5 minutes, then simmer for 15 minutes. Then allow the jam to cool for 15 minutes, removing any scum. Stir the strawberries carefully through the jam.

● Pot into warm jars, cover, label and date.

This type of jam will keep for up to 6 months.

— INGREDIENTS —

MAKES 1.4 KG

1.4 kg/3lb strawberries

1.4 kg/3lb sugar with pectin

juice and rind of ½ lemon

ROSE PETAL JAM

*H*enley-on-Thames is the true home of this very distinctive flavoured jam. Taught to me by my dear friend, Sue Webb, once you have made this you will be making it for friends and relatives all the time. Only pick the roses when they are in full blossom, carefully removing the petals and snipping off any white bases.

— INGREDIENTS —

450g/1lb rose heads

900g/2lb jam sugar with pectin

2 litres water

juice of 4 lemons

— METHOD —

● Place the rose petals into a large, clean bowl. Add half the sugar, cover with cling film and leave overnight in a warm place. This extracts the scent.

● Pour the water and lemon juice into a large saucepan, adding the remaining sugar, heat and cook until the sugar is completely dissolved (DO NOT BOIL).

● Add the rose petals stirring all the time, then simmer gently for 30 minutes. Bring to the boil for 3 minutes.

● Place into clean, warm jars, seal and cover and leave to stand for 7 days.

Regatta, Henley-upon-Thames, 1890.

LEMON CURD

his was served at lunch and tea, not just on bread and butter but in cakes and my mother's cheesecakes. For a Lime Curd, simply replace the lemons with fresh limes.

— INGREDIENTS —

MAKES 900G/2LB
4 large lemons,
juice and grated rind

225g/8oz butter, softened

450g/1lb castor sugar

5 large eggs, beaten

— METHOD —

● Place the lemon juice and grated rind into a bowl over a saucepan of boiling water, or a double saucepan.

● Whisk in the softened butter and sugar, whisking gently over a low heat until the mixture is completely dissolved.

● Take the pan from the heat and allow it to cool for 30 seconds. Whisk in the beaten eggs. Return the pan to the heat and cook gently again for 5 to 8 minutes, until the curd coats the back of the spoon.

● Pot and seal the curd.

Frodingham, Humberside, 1904.

BLACKCURRANT & PORT JAM

*U*se your favourite currant or berries for this recipe.

—— METHOD ——

● Put the blackcurrants into a large saucepan with the sugar and leave it for 2 hours. Simmer gently for 30 minutes until the sugar is completely dissolved. Add the port and bring to the boil, simmer for 15 minutes, let the jam stand for 15 minutes, then re-boil rapidly for 5 minutes.

● Pot and seal in warm jars. Allow the jam to mature for at least 14 days before use.

This jam can be used with venison or any other game where you normally use cranberry sauce.

—— INGREDIENTS ——

1.4kg/3lb blackcurrants, stalks removed

1kg/2lb sugar with pectin

150ml/¼ pint vintage port

Measuring the Hops,
Paddock Wood, c.1955.

YORKSHIRE ROWAN JELLY

he rowan berries must be just ripe and the apples sweet and ripe.

— INGREDIENTS —

900g/2lb rowan berries

900g/2lb Cox's orange pippin

water to cover

2kg/4½lb sugar with pectin

— METHOD —

• Remove any stalks from the rowan berries then wash and drain them.

• Peel, core and chop the apples.

• Place the fruits into a large saucepan and just cover them with water. Cook for 15 minutes then strain the fruit and liquid through a fine sieve into another clean saucepan.

• Add the sugar and pectin. Boil rapidly for 15 minutes until the jelly is nearly at setting point. Pot and seal in warm jars.

This is excellent with any of the game recipes throughout this book.

Market Place, Ripon, 1901.

ORANGE & WHISKEY MARMALADE

A taste of County Antrim, Northern Ireland, and a whiskey spelt with an 'e' from the Old Bushmills Distillery Co Ltd, which was first granted its licence to make this famous whiskey in 1608. Should you like lime marmalade replace the oranges with fresh limes and replace the whiskey with kirsch. For a true Oxford Marmalade omit the whiskey and cut the orange rind into thicker strips.

METHOD

- Wash the oranges and with a very sharp knife, carefully remove the rind, leaving the white coating pith on the oranges.

- Cut the orange rind into 5mm/¼ inch strips and place into the preserving pan with the juice squeezed from the oranges.

- Add the lemon juice and spring water, bring to the boil and reduce by half by simmering for at least 2 hours.

- Add the sugar with pectin and stir over a low heat until the sugar has dissolved. Bring to the boil rapidly for 20 minutes. Remove the pan from the heat and add the Irish whiskey.

- Blend thoroughly. Return to the heat and boil for a further 3 minutes. Carefully skim the marmalade and allow it to cool naturally for 20 minutes, before placing into clean jars.

INGREDIENTS

900g/2lb Seville oranges

juice of 1 lemon

2 litres of spring water

1.5kg/3lb sugar with pectin

5 tablespoons of Irish whiskey

PICCALILLI

his is a simple and effective way of using up the end of season vegetables. Today we can get these vegetables all year round.

— INGREDIENTS —

900g/2lb equal mixture of the following vegetables cut into bite size pieces: small cucumbers or gherkins, baby onions (peeled) and cauliflower florets

75g/3oz cooking salt

600ml/20floz white vinegar

175g/6oz granulated sugar

50g/2oz dried English mustard powder

1 teaspoon turmeric

25g/1oz cornflour

— METHOD —

● Put the vegetables into a large dish and sprinkle with the salt, cover and leave it to stand for 24 hours.

● Wash and rinse the vegetables. In a separate, large saucepan put the vinegar and heat it gently, then add the vegetables.

● Mix together all the dried ingredients and add to the vegetables and the vinegar, stir and simmer gently for 15 minutes.

CLARKE WITH AN E'S PICKLED ONIONS

I make my pickled onions quite sweet and I also use a milder vinegar than spiced or pickling vinegar. I find white wine vinegar less tangy and the use of soft brown sugar mellows the sharpness of the pickles. A friend of mine uses the same method for his pickled eggs, it is quite easy but Clarke always says use free range and they must be fresh. Slowly boil 1 dozen for 10 minutes, plunging them into cold water for at least 12 minutes, shell, wash again and they are ready for use.

METHOD

● To make a spiced vinegar add, 8 cloves 12g/$\frac{1}{2}$oz pieces of ginger and cinnamon with 8 white peppercorns to 1litre of malt vinegar. Bottle for 2 months and shake the bottle every week.

● Strain and use when required.

● Put all the ingredients into a glass bowl and stir with a wooden spoon until the sugar dissolves.

● Pack the pickles into jars and top up with the vinegar. Seal with vinegar proof tops and leave them to stand for at least 4 to 6 weeks before using them.

INGREDIENTS

900g/2lb pickling onions, peeled

600ml/20fl oz spiced or pickling vinegar, hot but not boiling

100g/4oz soft brown sugar

12g/$\frac{1}{2}$oz salt

1 teaspoon pink peppercorns

CLARKE'S PICKLED QUAIL EGGS

This is an ordinary vinegar method, which also using quail eggs. The eggs should be boiled for 6 minutes, stirring them after the first 2 minutes to centralise the yolks. Then plunge them into cold water for 6 minutes.

— INGREDIENTS —

12 fresh quail eggs, hard boiled and shelled

600ml/20floz white wine vinegar

3 blades mace

— METHOD —

- Pack the eggs into glass jars and cover with the vinegar, adding a blade of mace to each jar.

- Seal and leave for 1 month before using.

Cross Keys Hotel, Eppleby, Yorkshire, c.1955.

RED VELVET BEETROOT RELISH

*T*he finest beets in Britain come from the North of England. It is commonly known around Scarisbrick and Southport as Red Velvet country where hundreds of acres of very special beetroot are grown.

Serve this with chunks of your favourite cheese and my grandmother's home-made brown bread and butter (see recipe on page 183).

— METHOD —

- Simply place all the ingredients into a large saucepan, bring the pan to the boil slowly and allow the ingredients to infuse (stand) for 30 minutes. Return the saucepan to the heat and simmer gently for 30 minutes.

- Spoon the beetroot relish into clean, warm jars. Cover and seal with vinegar proof tops.

- Store in a cool, dry, dark place and leave to mature for 6 weeks.

— INGREDIENTS —

900g/2 lb Red Velvet cooked beetroot, diced

450g/1lb white cabbage, finely shredded

1 large onion, finely shredded

75g/3oz fresh horseradish, finely grated

1 teaspoon English mustard powder

600ml/1 pint red wine vinegar

225g/8oz brown sugar

100g/4oz sultanas

pinch grated nutmeg

salt

freshly milled black pepper

YORKSHIRE RELISH

*O*ne of the oldest preserves in Yorkshire history. In the inns and restaurants, if meat was covered with gravy the Yorkshireman became very suspicious, thinking it was yesterday's left-overs warmed up. They would ask for cold beef with a sauceboat of Yorkshire Relish.

— INGREDIENTS —

600ml/20floz malt vinegar

100g/4oz soft brown sugar

1 teaspoon salt

6 black peppercorns

25g/1oz chopped chillies

1 tablespoon black treacle

1 tablespoon Worcestershire sauce

1 tablespoon mushroom ketchup

½ teaspoon freshly grated nutmeg

— METHOD —

● Place all the ingredients into a saucepan and bring to the boil. Simmer for 10 minutes, allow the relish to cool.

● Pour into warm, clean bottles with corks or vinegar proof tops.

● This relish will keep for about 18 months if stored in a dry, dark place and will mature with age.

Viaducts & Boating, Knaresborough, 1921.

TRADITIONAL WHISKEY SAUCE

*I*t is simple to forget the easy things in life!

— METHOD —

- Mix the yolks, sugar and Whisky in a large clean bowl.

- Whisk on the boiled milk.

- Return the sauce to the saucepan and re-heat, stirring all the time with a wooden spoon on a very low heat. DO NOT BOIL or the eggs will scramble.

- At the very end add a little double cream, for extra creaminess.

— INGREDIENTS —

2 fresh egg yolks

25g/1oz castor sugar

45ml/3 tablespoons of single malt whisky

300ml/10floz fresh milk (hot)

— CHEF'S ALTERNATIVE TIP —

*For a Christmas **Brandy Sauce** omit the Whisky and add 45ml/3 tablespoons of brandy or rum custard, Simply add 30ml/2 tablespoons of your favourite tipple at the end of cooking and whisk gently before serving.*

Holyrood Palace, Arthur's Seat, 1887.

RED CABBAGE

Choose a really firm cabbage, removing any discoloured leaves. Cut the cabbage into quarters and cut out the inner stalk.

— INGREDIENTS —

1 red cabbage, washed and shredded

100g/4oz cooking salt

50g/2oz soft brown sugar

600ml/20floz white wine vinegar

— METHOD —

• Place the shredded cabbage, salt and sugar into layers in a large basin, cover with cling film and leave it to stand for 24 hours.

• Rinse the cabbage in cold water, draining it well. Pack the cabbage quite loosely into jars, cover with the white wine vinegar and seal.

• Let the red cabbage stand for at least 7 days before using and use within 3 months, or it will lose its crispness.

Dorcester Road, Maiden Norton, Dorset, 1906.

BEETROOT & RHUBARB CHUTNEY

*T*his is very much a taste of the Lancashire hills, an exciting taste, ideal for game.

— METHOD —

● Put all the ingredients into a large saucepan, bring to the boil and simmer slowly for 10 minutes, stirring all the time. Then let the mixture stand for 30 minutes. Bring back to the boil and simmer for 30 minutes.

● Put into warm jars and let it stand for 3 weeks before using.

Woolacombe, 1885.

— INGREDIENTS —

450g/1lb Red Velvet cooked beetroot, diced

450g/1lb rhubarb, (red end) washed and chopped

2 onions, chopped

3 tablespoons sultanas

1 tablespoon green peppercorns in brine

4 tablespoons soft brown sugar

pinch cayenne pepper

1 teaspoon salt

1 tablespoon mild curry paste

2 tablespoons port

150ml/5floz white wine vinegar

STRAWBERRY VINEGAR

his is my idea of a tasty summer vinegar, for using with baby beetroot or blended with a little olive oil and English mustard for a summer salad dressing.

INGREDIENTS

900g/2lb fresh strawberries

2 litre white wine vinegar

900g/2lb granulated sugar

METHOD

● Put the hulled strawberries into a large, clean glass bowl. Pour over enough vinegar to cover the strawberries. Cover and leave them to stand for 4 days, stirring every day.

● Strain the liquid through a non-metallic sieve, being very careful not to crush the strawberries through the sieve as this will make the vinegar cloudy. Pour the juice into a saucepan, add the sugar, bring the juice to the boil and then simmer for 20 minutes.

● Let the liquid stand until it is completely cold and then bottle, using cork or plastic tops. Seal and let it stand for at least 4 days before use.

● You can use this same method and recipe with any soft fruit berries.

The Centre Court, The Park, Wimbledon, c.1950.

INDEX

INDEX

INDEX